HIDDEN LIGHTS

HIDDEN LIGHTS

A Collection of

TRUTHS

Not Often Told

EDITED BY
CAROLYN RIKER & BETHANNE KAPANSKY WRIGHT

FIRST PRINT EDITION, September 2017
FIRST EBOOK EDITION, September 2017

Copyright © 2017 by
BethAnne Kapansky Wright & Carolyn Riker Avalani

Cover Art by BethAnne Kapansky Wright.
Chapter illustrations by BethAnne Kapansky Wright.
Artwork on pages 226 and 228 by Lucy M. Radatz.
Photographs on pages v and 241 by Jean-Louis Latil.

All rights reserved.

First published in the United States of America
by Golden Dragonfly Press, 2017.

No part of this document may be reproduced or transmitted in any form
or by any means, electronic or otherwise,
without prior written permission by the copyright owner.

www.goldendragonflypress.com

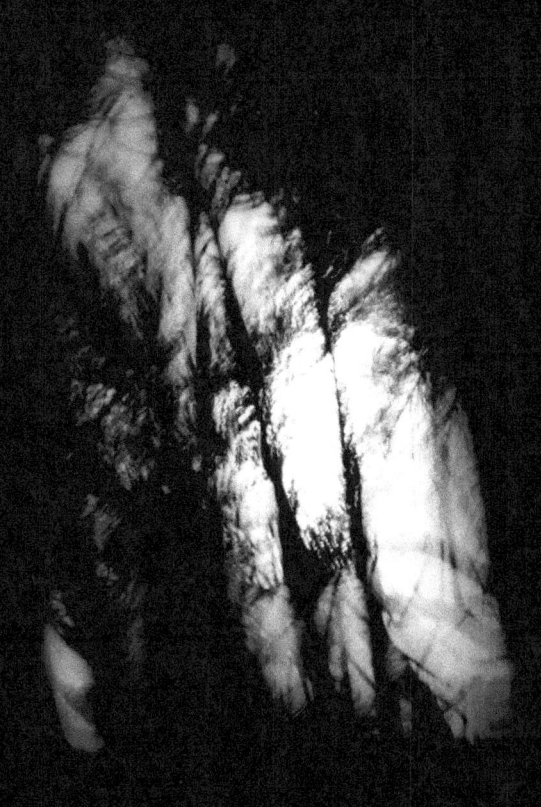

*"There are no unsacred places;
there are only sacred places
and desecrated places."*

—Wendell Berry

CONTENTS

Introduction	1

CHAPTER 1
I Belong

The Caretaker Cindy Burrill	7
Keep Making Your Life Your Own Annie Dear	8
Homelands Hillary Walker	9
Older Sisters Robin Baldwin	10
The Smoky Scent of Abandon Nancy Shiner	11
AWAY, I FLY Sonja Phillips	13
Creation Kathryn Brown Ramsperger	14
Silencing Along the Stormy Shore Nancy Shiner	15
Peripheral Jody Kristine Johnson	17
Portia Sean Ramsperger	18
Cravings Taylar Nuevelle	19
The Cliff Jody Kristine Johnson	21

CHAPTER 2
I Grieve

	23
Weep With Those Who Weep Annie Dear	25
Tangerine Sunset BethAnne Kapansky Wright	27
If I Planted a Rainbow Maureen Kwiat Meshenberg	29
Abandonment Dolly Mahtani	31
I Hear Her in the Rain Catherine L. Schweig	34
Broken Vrinda Aguilera	36
Suriyya Begum Nadia Iqbal	38
Mother Sherry L Jonckheere	42

The Chapel of Dis-Enlightenment   Cari Greywolf   43
Sweeter Than Honey?   Julia W. Prentice   45
I See Her Glow Now   Maureen Kwiat Meshenberg   47
La Luna in Every Stage   Olivia Delgado   49
My Life as I Know It at Ten Years Old   Carmel Breathnach   51
Grief's Love   Carolyn Riker   53

CHAPTER 3   55
I Am Worthy

I Claim My Space   Jennifer Jepson   57
Keep on Keeping   Annie Dear   58
Away From the Sun   India R. Adams   60
The Beloved Within   Lauren Love   61
Ordinary Sees Extraordinary   Carolyn Riker   63
Goddess Incarnate   Shilo Quetchenbach   64
The Bear's Savaging   Nancy Shiner   66
A Life Called Survival   Mariann Martland   68
My Mother has a Mirror   Judi Lenehan   69
Winged Dream   Olivia Delgado   71
At the Bottom   Lisa Antley   72
The Unspeakable Act   Cari Greywolf   73
Grounded   Mariann Martland   75
We are Worthy   Carolyn Riker   77

CHAPTER 4   79
I am Seen

Upper Mind Strength   Jody Kristine Johnson   81
Eggshell Stomping   Annie Dear   82
Unsolicited Advice   Marianne Pownall   83
Disappearance & Other Acts of Magic   Shannon Crossman   85
My Writing Room   Nancy Shiner   87

Stilted Judi Lenehan	89
Pelos: This Body of Mine SK Lockhart	90
WANT Jaymz Hawkes	92
Safeguard the Goodness Within Annie Dear	94
Self-Identity Slowly Rises Don R. Johnson	95
Collecting Pieces of Her Ilda Dashi	96
Nothing Was Ever Enough SK Lockhart	97
The Treachery of Breadcrumbs Jennifer C. Zechlin	99

CHAPTER 5
Love is Love
101

Jessica's Story Jessica Wicks	103
My Voice is Getting Clearer Jhilmil Breckenridge	106
Queer Enough Shilo Quetchenbach	107
Trans Women: A Sonnet Margo Stebbing	109
But I'm a Man Ryan Dumas	110
TRANSSEPARATION Jessica Wicks	112
Bending Reality Dolly Mahtani	116
The Twice-Given Gift T.J. Banks	118

CHAPTER 6
Unseen Scars
121

Forever Asleep Alice Maldonado Gallardo	123
Before It's Too Late Angel Garmon	125
Consent SK Lockhart	127
Out to Sea Sherry L Jonckheere	129
Collage of Scars Alice Maldonado Gallardo	130
Silence Perpetuates Abuse Carolyn Riker	131
(My Abusers) Did You Know? Mariann Martland	132
The Bloodletting Ritual Nancy Shiner	133
Finding Safety Margo Stebbing	135

Crimson SK Lockhart	137
The Anxiety That Holds Mariann Martland	138
The Empath Anthem Dolly Mahtani	139
Say What You Need To Say Annie Dear	141

CHAPTER 7   143
We Are Her Protectors

At The Edge of a Season Anita Acuna	145
Farthest Reach BethAnne Kapansky Wright	146
Beneath the Surface Jody Kristine Johnson	148
Extinction BethAnne Kapansky Wright	149
If We Could Turn Back Time/Doomsday Kai Coggin	151
Autumn Haikus Anita Acuna	155
Home Kathryn Brown Ramsperger	156
Fleeting Judi Lenehan	157
Deconstructing Darwin Cari Greywolf	158
Inshallah Margo Stebbing	159
Duwamish Judi Lenehan	161
Song of Oshun Anita Acuna	162
Habitat BethAnne Kapansky Wright	164

CHAPTER 8   167
I Believe

Circle of Women Robin Baldwin	169
She Who Will Fly Tammy T. Stone	170
The Reluctant Shaman BethAnne Kapansky Wright	171
Ancient Hymns of Her Sonja Phillips	173
The Wall That Divides Me from Myself Ilda Dashi	174
Trust Me on This Robin Baldwin	176
Unveiling the Mystery Sonja Phillips	178
We are Women Robin Baldwin	179

Dogma Molly Moblo Perusse	180
An Attitude of Gratitude Dolly Mahtani	182
The Child Within Needs Gentle Care Annie Dear	183
Crossroads Robin Baldwin	184
Addiction Kathryn Brown Ramsperger	185
Battle Cry Sherry L Jonckheere	186

CHAPTER 9 — 189
Justice Speaks

I'll Write a Song Carolyn Riker	191
After the Election Linda Webber	192
Still (in two parts) Kai Coggin	193
Days of Dickens and Hobbes Cari Greywolf	196
Voices of Truth Carolyn Riker	198
Day 1: In Response to T.S. Eliot Margo Stebbing	199
We Will Come To Love Maureen Kwiat Meshenberg	202
Those Geese Are Mean Sherry L Jonckheere	203
Breaking the Silence Beverly Collier	204
Where Democracy Rises Carolyn Riker	206
Declaration Sean Ramsperger	207
Walls in Midair Kai Coggin	208

CHAPTER 10 — 211
We Are the Change

I Will No Longer be Kept Silent Carolyn Riker	213
Truth and Reconciliation for Two Wings Margo Stebbing	215
WHERE THE ANGELS FLY Sonja Phillips	218
Mercy India Elaine Holland-Garnett	219
Choices Cindy Burrill	220
Empathy BethAnne Kapansky Wright	221
Surreal Reality Robin Baldwin	223

Tangible Hope April M. Lee	225
Artist Statement Lucy M. Radatz	227
13 Stars//It Takes All 50 Lucy M. Radatz	229
INNER POET Sonja Phillips	231
Windows Kai Coggin	232
Some of Us Are Just Awakening Maureen Kwiat Meshenberg	233
Freedom Song BethAnne Kapansky Wright	235
We Can Change Anything Tracie Nichols	238
Acknowledgments	241
About the Authors	243
About the Editors	255

INTRODUCTION

"Many stories matter. Stories have been used to dispossess and to malign. But stories can also be used to empower and to humanize. Stories can break the dignity of a people. But stories can also repair that broken dignity."

—Chimamanda Ngozi Adich

This anthology was birthed out of the oppressive, 2016 USA Presidential Campaign and the rise of increased violence to annihilate people's stories often unheard or seen. After the election, we found ourselves in a similar heart-soul space of grief, loss, anger, and a burgeoning desire to give voice to truth and authenticity. Real is needed in this world.

After rallying against an intense, initial inertia, we each felt compelled to begin anthology projects that spoke the truth. As our projects grew, and our paths intersected, we realized we were working on the same vision and decided to combine forces.

In the compilation of this anthology, we have been touched, teary-eyed, astounded and humbled by the stories that poured in. What a privilege and honor it has been to witness such tremendous words and to see them come together to create *Hidden Lights*. We are no longer hidden but seen and heard and believed.

When we speak our truth, it creates room for more truth. Each story told in these pages is a stepping stone for us as individuals and for us as a collective. There's a fuller and clearer whole picture grafted by the stained glass of our diversity; it is gathered here, in these pages, where all voices are treasured, witnessed, and respected.

Hidden Lights is a book of realness. It is a collaboration of over 50 experienced and novice writers sharing their stories, poems, and prose from around the globe. The poignancy of each piece covers the depths and widths of human experiences. Some are raw and raging, while others are gentle. However, each piece is riveting and insightful; words that plunge from the veins of souls.

We've kept, as close as possible, the writing style of each contributor. There are 10 chapters that describe the bittersweet of humanity by crossing over stereotypes of gender and racial decree. Touching alongside the power of suicide. Hearing the outcry of justice. Holding the strength of despair and depression and grief. The final two chapters: Justice Speaks and We are the Change, are the clarion call for a deeper truth sought by our various voices. Thusly, wrapping an inclusiveness in the cusp of being seen and heard.

The message is clear:

We are all needed. We are all stronger in our diversity. We are all a part of the whole.

With Respect and Love,
Carolyn and BethAnne

"We must believe in the power and strength of our words. Our words can change the world."

MALALA YOUSAFZAI

CHAPTER 1

I BELONG

*"Loving ourselves
through the process of owning our own story
is the bravest thing we'll ever do."*
—Brené Brown

The Caretaker
Cindy Burrill

Exhaustion.
Dreams of nothingness.
Dreams of silent abandonment
from all those around me.

Treasured roles —
Daughter
Mother
Grandmother
Friend
Neighbor
Student
Employee

A need to be needed.

Needed.
Silent screams for freedom
that which fills me,
depletes me.
That which completes me,
breaks me.

Lukewarm
An identity lost in a fog
of who I once was.
Blinded by the reality
of who I am.

Visions of solitude
shielded by a panic of isolation.

A quest to evolve
in a shadow of complacency.

The illusion of distance.
Close, yet far away.
Challenged to face the unknown.
An unchartered path to selfhood.
Endless possibilities for a life yet lived.

Keep Making Your Life Your Own

Annie Dear

am I the captain of my soul?
not yet, no, not yet
but wound by wound
and indignity by indignity
and boundary by boundary
I am reframing
and rebuffing
and retaking control
and the negative of my life
is being redeveloped
and the black is become
white and the white
is become a being
I am learning to own
and soft words are being
offered for harsh words
long-time still told
and affirmation and joy
are being freely given
by hearts that do not withhold
and new voices begin to
overrule the painful voices
of old and one day, some day
I think the day
will finally come
when I am indeed
the captain of my soul.

Homelands

Hillary Walker

Love for me was always across la frontera. Demarcations. Sometimes enemy lines. I did not know how to hold myself, how to keep safe against the mange wolf and the sun sear and saying yes but meaning no.

No matter how many times I consulted the map, I could not divine water. I sensed deep wells, but my spade returned dry. You cannot carry your spirit in a canteen. You cannot live off the preferences of others forever.

One day, you must return home.

In the morning, I drank coffee with him under *los gigantes* and thought of their other names. Elephant cactus, *cardón*, *Pachycereus pringlei*. I named all the words we have for love.

Sometimes in the car, his hand moved over my thigh. Sometimes I was holding my breath, waiting for the other shoe to drop. Rain interrupted a three-year drought. The arroyo opened with color. On the crumpled map, I traced back over the miles of highway—the beginning and the words hard for my mouth to say and how I had always felt twelve inches to the left of my own body and sometimes hundreds of miles further back. I cast my hand through the window to feel the moving desert air. I cast my face to the sun. When I saw caves in the hill, I wanted my voice to stir the darkness inside them. I wanted to holler and whoop and say anything that would return as a message from the other side.

"Let's stop," is what I said.

Suddenly untamed.

Here I was all along.

Older Sisters
Robin Baldwin

Some people collect stamps,
Or coins and even wine.
Me? I collect older sisters.
They are my wise souls
Who have offered me
Windows into their worlds,
Teaching me life,
Showing me love,
Encouraging me always.
These women are strong,
Forging their paths in this world.
These women are funny,
Laughing at themselves,
These women are genuine,
Caring for others so deeply.
I am grateful that God
Brought them to me,
Recognizing their beauty
And the gifts they would bestow
As they each taught me something
About myself that I didn't know.
I am who I am today
Because of them.

The Smoky Scent of Abandon
Nancy Shiner

There is no greater loneliness than the moment you recognize that your "Enough" will never be enough. That all the hoping and praying and wishing that someone will find you worthy of their love, their time, their willingness to claim you as part of their own, has evaporated in air like a wisp of stale smoke from a lone cigar. The *having* of you equally appealing as the spent butt they discard upon the floor.

And with heel pressed firmly on littered trash, you too feel the discard of unwanted self as they walk away, not even a backwards glance to observe your last dying ember.

My soul turned to ash by the countless discarding of nicotine-stained hearts.

Loneliness is painful—more painful than the acerbic sting of razor pulled across tightened skin that screams in protest your inevitable leaving. As raw and bloodied heart is eaten alive from the inside out, while entrails scatter about my feet and stain the footprints that trail your final retreat.

My heart becomes deadened, as to allow it to beat, in the face of this abandon and would force its bleeding out to destroy a body numbed in the defense of this shaming.

Ahhhh, the shame! Now that's a force to be reckoned with.

For how else to explain the ease with which you walked away, but to gaze at the reflection that hides in the mirror and recognizes the monster staring back? If I were human, would you want me still? But I lost my humanity long ago as to stand in the presence of such overwhelming want—is to die daily so as to prevent the knowing that you have long since ceased to live. *My skin starving in the absence of human touch.*

I will not want you back! I cry. Yet it is you that owns the not wanting.

Loneliness is an evil mate as it cleaves itself body and soul to your side—a nasty lover whose loyalty demands complete and utter compliance. In the end, the very wishing for all you cannot have, leaves you gasping for breath in the reality of all you have never received.

And as a gust of wind picks up ruined stump and carelessly tosses it into the trash, I too claim the truth of my complete negation of worth. There will be no reigniting of my innards. In the absence of your seeing me, I have ceased to exist.

AWAY, I FLY
Sonja Phillips

I could never be
a part of someone else's love story
I deserve my own.
I desire more

than just your empty words
of nightly confessions
leaked by your fictitious pen
unlike her, I let go.
She kept forgiving you

until there was nothing left
the one you hold so dear
oblivious to the one
you claim to love,
envious of the one
you can't live without.
When truth lies down

with darkness
she uncovers a multitude of sins
so many roses in your garden,
not enough [love] to go around.
So many butterflies

with broken wings.
Away, I fly
I could never be caged.
I must write my own story
A wise woman covered in her wounds

knows when love is real
love sets her spirit free.

Creation

Kathryn Brown Ramsperger

She lives in the park.
When it rains, she crouches under benches.
When it snows, she hides in subway corners.
She is small and dark like a mouse's shadow.
She carries a feather pillow and a parasol,
And wears clothes in layers,
And does not speak the language well.
She knows "help" and "money."
The drifters drift past her.
Only yesterday I wondered
If problems were human in creation,
Meaningless
Beside infinity.
She is blind.
But I see a universe behind those eyes.

Silencing Along the Stormy Shore

Nancy Shiner

Having a voice in the face of a lifetime of secrets is highly discouraged. In the silencing of your story there is eventually a revolt, as the rage within at this denial overwhelms. In the need to speak your truth—the tug of war between owning it, and drowning in its muzzling—can be an epic battle. A battle that if not emerged from triumphant, can drown you in its turbulent struggle.

The rage erupts like waves crashing onto the shore with a fury that beats its tempo unto the sand. Begun as a pebble dropped into the water's silent face, it begins a ripple that spreads like skipping stone in ever-widening circles until it encompasses the breadth and depth of the ocean's frame. This surface, vehemence, a mere tip of the iceberg that indicates its bottomless expanse.

My body is that ocean of white-hot rage and my inner being the captive craft that contains its seething mutiny. I have no means by which to batten my fortress against the frenzy that causes the sand to retreat against its violent assault. *No protection for the shore so beaten back from storms of past.* Thus, the erosion of boundary's edge swallows the coast as it is pummeled by whitecaps that claim the water's edge. It bows down in defeat as its grains of sand are swept away to the calling of a master that shouts its fury into the night. My heart the altar that lays prostrate on the sandy shore in offering to the gods of primal rage and terror.

I will be claimed by the ocean tonight and drowned in the waters that carry my body to its turbulent depths. I, as sacrificial lamb to quiet the deities whose awareness of my ever-growing tempestuous nature must be appeased. Divinity of all that was taken from me—a totem to the nature of humanity's shameful lust. My body, the subsidy for others' lascivious nature.

So, I lay still in the heartbeat between the rhythmic waves' crashing upon the shore. And, I time my breath to the pulse of its undulating fists that pound the rocky berm. As I wait in silent surrender for the surge to sweep me out to its salty brine. This sting of salt upon my lips, a familiar tang.

A burial by sea. No Taps to be played.

A simple surrender to the water's furious tempo and its violent demand that my emerging voice be silenced.

Peripheral

Jody Kristine Johnson

I live on the edges of people's lives,
not allowed in the center
where everything happens
where all is decided
They see me when I'm there in front of them;
they laugh at my jokes
and compliment my sweater
but I am not invited to their birthday parties
and they don't show up at mine
When I'm not there
they go on with their lives
and look surprised when I return
as if suddenly reminded
that I still exist in their world,
at least tangentially.
I live on the edges of people's lives
not quite allowed to enter their hearts and minds
not quite like them—
a subtle outcast: an afterthought
an image that doesn't burn
into their soul or inspire their hearts;
a nonpermanent dye
that fades with each washing.

Portia

Sean Ramsperger

Rich, beautiful and breathtaking
Everything you would ever want
The highest of all heroines
She is her own star shining in the sky
By Destiny blocked to choose her own path

Trapped by the law
More than just beauty behind her
Wanting only to find who she loves
Prettying herself up
To see the next suitor pass by

Many men choosing wrong
Only looking on the outside
Sad to see she is not all silver and gold
Yet later wishing they could have gotten to know her
But it is too late, and reality hits them hard.

For she is intelligent, brave and witty
A genius hidden by splendor
Yet there is nothing she can do for herself
Since society prevents and entraps her
She cannot be what every woman wants
to be Free.

Cravings
Taylar Nuevelle

June 2014 Secure Female Facility (SFF) Hazelton.
What I've learned is that FREEDOM is not about being unlocked and unwatched. Freedom is a series of things enjoyed, despised, earned, given without restrictions, and so much more.

- Cold, peeled mangoes sliced lengthwise or in fat cubes; juice springing freely over my tongue and slip sliding down my throat.
- Arguing with someone I choose to be around and not fear being locked away while I am already locked up.
- Peeing in a separate place from where I sleep and eat. Peeing alone as opposed to having someone on my right, left, and down the way from me. Ditto for pooping.
- A very tiny sundress, with spaghetti straps and high, high strappy heels that click on the concrete as I walk my fast walk through the city.
- The sound of the Metro approaching and the lady's voice trapped in the box forever announcing, "Doors closing."
- Regular flavored Bubble Yum bubble gum bursting with so much sugar my teeth ache just remembering. Blowing bubbles inside of bubbles and the kids clapping and screaming, "More Auntie, more," because I am so silly and can blow bubbles inside of bubbles, even though I am long past grown up.
- Shrimp Tempura sushi from the Japanese place just off of DuPont Circle on 19th Street. Maguro Tuna over rice that melts on my tongue and stings from too much wasabi sauce.
- Hugs from E that cover not only my body, but my soul.
- Waking to the "Beep. Beep. Beep." Of my coffee maker announcing with its sound and smell that it is time to get up and drink my Café Du Monde coffee—all the way from New

Orleans, but purchased cheaply at the Vietnamese grocery store in Falls Church, Virginia.

- ☙ Pho Ga. Cha Gio rolls. Vietnamese coffee. Pork grilled over noodles laced with fish sauce.
- ☙ Red wine. Red wine. Red wine. Red wine. Red wine. Red wine. Red Wine.
- ☙ Staring without reason or need to do otherwise at my books living their lives on my lovely bookshelves.
- ☙ Long, endless walks through independently owned bookstores. Touching, stroking, and smelling the books. Lingering over beautifully designed covers, allowing all worldly cares to disappear.
- ☙ *My son's voice. My son. It is not enough to say. Touching my son is freedom.*
- ☙ Fat brother showing up, unannounced demanding beer and food.
- ☙ Baby brother's lazy way of being that just eases everything and allows me to laugh without inhibition.
- ☙ My niece's voice. My niece. It is not enough to say. *Touching my niece is freedom.*
- ☙ Short, extra dry full fat cappuccinos. Baking in a real oven. Laughter heard by those who love me. Crying alone. Singing aloud.

Freedom is a prayer without hope, because the prayer is already answered.

The Cliff
Jody Kristine Johnson

Most of the time my mind carries
the weight of what I am,
the knowledge that what I need the most
is missing
the fear that there is no relief for me
because of how I was made;
no hope for a reprieve.
I balance the weight
against my love for my children
my devotion to my dog
the meaning in my work
the dear faces and hearts of my cherished friends
but there are times when the weight slips,
when I am not as strong
times when I am tired or sick
discouraged or in pain
and the full enormous pressure of what I carry
comes crashing down on me
a mental lumbar strain that leaves me gasping
on the ground
pinned beneath my own despair
writhing with the unrelenting knowledge
that I cannot change what I am;
and what I am is not enough to inspire love.

CHAPTER 2

I GRIEVE

*"Walking with a friend in the dark
is better than walking alone in the light."*
—Helen Keller

Weep With Those Who Weep
Annie Dear

and today
the need to cry
is strong
and my tears line up
ready to fall
but they don't
long years of training
hold them in thrall:
 'don't rock the boat
it's not that bad
worse things happen at sea
at least you're not dead
no need to make a fuss and
the silencing coup de grace
what about the children
starving in Africa?'
and I think of the children
hurt by the world
hungry in Africa
sick in America
bombed in Syria
abandoned in India
ill-treated in shame
ignored in good faith
and starved for loves
outpouring
the wide world round
and I open my heart
to the pain of it all
and impotence
strikes me anew
and the need to cry

is strong
and my tears line up
hot and heavy
and I long for them
to fall
and I wonder
if they will.

Tangerine Sunset

BethAnne Kapansky Wright

Lately, feelings flow through me like water. In and out in swishing churns, so many things swirling, I can't hold onto any single one. Uncontainable. I just let them swish.

Stress, anxiety, leave-taking. Disappointment, hurt, displacement. A sense of things unraveling swiftly, yet not swift enough. Presence, wonder, brushes of spring. A soft savor of the molecule of a moment —*last night's tangerine sunset, today's soft pink rise.*

Disquiet and quiet and fatigue underneath it all that just keeps getting tamped down in endless streams of things to do.

Swish, swoosh…my multitudes lap in gentle ebbs and flows.

I talk to the trees and the sky even more these days. Transitioning between two worlds—one life unforming, another not yet formed—I don't know where I fit anymore other than knowing *I always have a place in earth's arms, always find a counterpart against the trunk of a kind tree who says it's okay to be still and not know for a while.*

I work on building the bridge that will take me from Alaska to Hawaii, even as I struggle over the labor and wish the equipment operated with more ease. Kauai is drawing closer, and I keep wondering who I'll be there. How life will look without endless streams of things to do? How I will look with more space to breathe? *What mysteries the land holds for me.*

This time last year, I was wandering underneath the same patch of sky, talking to the same trees, trying to find solace in their whispers. Brent is dead, and I've lost my place. I didn't fit then either. Nobody knew what to say to me—how to help.

Nature became my medicine. Spirit my kindred. Earth my container.

She holds me now. Reminds me of the rich diversity in this world and how she's big enough to hold our all. Reminds me our whole is bigger than the sum of our parts. Reminds me I'm big enough to hold my all. Reminds me change is life's way.

I'm learning a lot about myself in the molecules of these moments. That you can unravel and lose yourself many times over. Only to find your way each night in the truth of a tangerine sunset.

If I Planted a Rainbow
Maureen Kwiat Meshenberg

If I planted a rainbow,
would the colors rise—
into the crying sky,
like iridescent butterflies—
spreading their wings to,
touch yours,
feathers of grace and light.

If I planted a rainbow,
will the colors fade—
with pain and ache,
or will they be—
watered by the tears,
of the many who loved you—
causing its radiance,
to light our sky—
with brilliant love rising.

If I planted a rainbow,
on 49 graves—
will the colors blend,
with yours—
your beauty,
your smile,
entering the earth—
sorrow mingled with memory,
taking the pain,
blending it with your love—
touching us,
touching the sun, moon and stars.

If I planted a rainbow,
will it allow the colors—
to flow into our souls,
holding our hearts with yours—
reminding us of you forever.

Poet's note: Written in memory of Orlando's Pulse Nightclub shooting, 2016.

Abandonment

Dolly Mahtani

I was nine years old when we found out that my grandmother had cancer. We flew 7,453 km to visit her. When my grandfather first saw me, he started yelling. I did not understand Hindi at 9 years old. All I knew was my mother was sobbing and my grandfather was yelling and I knew it had something to do with me.

"No granddaughter of mine can look like that, do you hear me? It's disrespectful. You have no pride. You're both disgusting," he continued to yell at my mother.

She wouldn't stop crying. I didn't know what to do. He looked at me with fury in his eyes, taking a few steps towards me as if he were going to strike me with the might of Zeus but my mother protected me. *She protected me. She stood in front of me like a human shield and defended me.* All of a sudden, all the fights we ever had, all the times she'd lock me out the house if I disobeyed her, all the threats, the times I ran away, the times she came looking for me, the times she didn't, none of it mattered anymore. She was here now. My mother was on my side for the first time. We both had a common enemy and we were united.

Later that night she told me I was going on a trip with my cousins to the mountains. She knew I really wanted to see them but she couldn't come and neither could my brother. Because of this, I didn't want to go. I wanted to stay with them. She insisted I go. She promised I'd have a good time and when I got back she'd be there with my brother waiting for me. I didn't like it but I knew I was going. By choice or by force. *I made her promise to all the gods she believed in that she would be there when I got back. She promised.*

The next morning, I stood at the top of the stairs of the entrance watching her walk down holding my brother's tiny little hand. I got a feeling in my gut. I started to cry incessantly.

She shed a tear too and opened the door. She turned back to look at me.

"Be good, okay? Don't trouble anyone. Listen to your aunt. Make me proud, okay? I'll see you soon! Love you." She said before the door closed.

Later that day I felt sick. We got back that same night exhausted from the trip. I didn't forget. I ran straight to my mother's room. She wasn't there. I ran to my room. My brother wasn't there. Where were they?

"They went out. They'll be back later," my aunt said.

I sat around anxiously waiting and fighting sleep. No matter how many times they told me to go to bed, that I'd see them in the morning, I had a bad gut feeling. I stayed awake. I stayed awake for as long as I could. When I woke up again I kept looking. They were nowhere to be found. I asked everyone. No one could tell me where they'd gone and why they weren't coming back. My aunt took me to my grandfather's office later that evening. She pat my back and left me in a chair opposite him. I was sad. Loose tears falling from my eyes every now and then.

"You want to know where your mother is?" he asked. I nodded.

"She left you. She doesn't want you. Look at you. You're fat, you're ugly. You don't listen. You're disgusting. You're a freeloader. I will teach you now, how to be worthy of being a part of this family. You will learn how to be decent and disciplined. You hear me? If you do not listen to me…." He proceeded to slap me across my face.

I had no idea why because he was speaking Hindi, however, the tone of his voice made my lower lip quiver as if an ocean of tears were ready to come bursting through my eyes. I tried to hold myself together. I had no idea what would happen otherwise. I was so scared of this man. I just wanted my mother. The known monster.

"Do you understand? Do you understand what I'm saying to you or are you stupid too?" he continued when he realized I wasn't reacting.

Finally, my aunt knelt down next to me and looked me in the eye.

"Sweetie, your mother and your brother had to go back home. You are going to stay here with me for a bit. She will come back when she can. We can call her later tonight, okay?"

"But she promised…" Even though I somehow knew at that moment. I knew she was going to break her promise before she ever made it. Just like she did all the others.

"What did she promise? Listen, everything will be okay. You just have to listen to me, okay? Listen to me and lose the weight so you can look pretty and make mama happy so when she comes she can see you nice and skinny and obedient and smiling, okay?"

That was the moment when I discovered my biggest fear had come true. My mother didn't love me. Because of that she left me and there was nothing I could do.

I Hear Her in the Rain

Catherine L. Schweig

Her premature death arrived the way a thunderstorm hits the valley of Mexico City: in sudden, dramatic shock that sends everyone running for cover. That's how it felt to me the summer Monica died. I was eleven. The adults fumbled with words, made themselves scarce and spoke of her only in ominous, hushed tones. This left me electric with unsatisfied questions that rumbled through my stomach like thunder, forming a trail of sleepless nights. One day Monica was happily playing tetherball with us neighborhood children, and the next morning her parents were making funeral arrangements for their firstborn child.

I usually found the adults approachable and welcoming of our questions. But the summer Monica died, they wore squished faces and taut spines, and dismissed me with a wave of their hands. Yet, it wasn't the first time a child's death had stunned our neighborhood. There had been the baby up the street who died in her crib one night. Her grieving mother averted tearful eyes from us children every time she would drive past our hopscotch games, trailing our white chalk on her tires, like clingy pain fed by avoidance.

I was beginning to conclude that adults dealt with death by burying it, pouring themselves extra cups of coffee in the mornings and generous glasses of chardonnay in the evenings. Then came the long awaited, feeble explanation, rolling off their knotted tongues like notes sung out of tune: Monica had died of an undetected brain aneurysm. She had died painlessly. She was now *in heaven*.

So it was, that my malnourished curiosity lingered. Having given up on the adults, I nibbled at the books in my father's study instead. There, sitting cross-legged on the rug, with an art book opened over my knees, I devoured a painting of Michelangelo's *The Last Judgment*. In the grand fresco that decorated the wall behind the Sistine Chapel altar—dripping with trumpets, serpent coils and skeletons—I saw mostly chaos and fear. There, in the half-naked figures, I thought I recognized familiar expressions: ones I had seen the adults around me wearing after Monica's unexpected departure, transparent in their terror of having one of their own children abruptly snatched away. Then it hit me: I was one such child.

The night before Monica's funeral I lay awake wondering if I might risk falling asleep and never wake up again. Or perhaps I would wake up but find myself in another location. Or I may simply cease existing altogether! Where was this "heaven" Monica had supposedly reached? As the storm clouds moved on and the clear August sky peered down at me through a sliver in my curtains, I imagined Monica among the stars, sending sparkling messages down to me in Morse code.

I didn't own a black dress. I was, after all, only a child. So I wore my cream-colored skirt with the soft, pink roses on it instead, and walked towards the coffin at the front of the church, clenching the white calla lily in my hand like my life depended on it. I thought seeing Monica's face again would help me crack death's code. And I pictured her laughing on our last night together. She had been beating me at tetherball. The white of her teeth lit up under the streetlight like the ivory on our piano keys did on sunny days. Having been neighbors, sometimes we could hear each other practicing. As I reached the front of the line, the piano playing in my head ended abruptly, for the casket was closed. Disappointed, I placed my flower atop it.

The following week I immersed myself in attempts to reach Monica, trying everything from fervent prayer to Ouija boards, restless in my inability to say goodbye. I didn't know how to release Monica, until one afternoon, when the piano keys called me over. I played and played, weaving lyrics that spoke directly to Monica into the melody. Finally, I sensed the possibility of reaching her through music. When the song was complete, I gathered my little sister and the rest of Monica's surviving girlfriends, and taught them the lyrics.

I hand-delivered concert invitations on colored construction paper. Monica's parents sat in the front seats with her little brother fidgeting by their side. When we were finished singing, I slid off the piano bench to face the audience, and all the adults were in tears. Something had softened in them. Shock and discomfort had been replaced with healthy grief. Cookies were passed around, and we spoke about Monica's short life. She was twelve when she died. I never knew if Monica heard the concert or not, but every now and then, when summer rains tap staccato-like on my roof, I'm pretty sure I hear the sound of her piano-playing mixed in with it.

Broken

Vrinda Aguilera

You, my rage. You who have been silently building up pressure like a subterranean, century's dormant volcano; you reared your heedless head today. Prodded awake from your slumber, you, my beast, awoke.

Eyes rolling and wild, frantically looking without seeing, you thrashed this way and that, searching for an enemy to ravage, to devour. Tiny flecks of froth and foam spitting here and there in your frenzy, you suffused me with your magnitude and I was lost.

Feet violently yanked out from under me, I found myself floundering and drowning in your salty waters. I gasped, desperately opened my mouth to inhale and, instead, sucked down gallon upon gallon of your black and murky brine. Choke cough sputtering, I exhaled, then swiftly vomited up searing orange blue flames. A dragon? Since when have I become a dragon?

A dragon. For now I breathe fire, yellow, bluish-red, licking and flickering flames embellished with decorative curlicue tendrils of white hot smoke. My shouting, yelling fire breath overtook me and burned. Oh, they burned, scalded and singed any and every unlucky soul in my path.

Along with myself. My angry exhalations gave vent to my Rage, Pain, and Fury. My voice an energetic vehicle for these unruly passengers hell bent on joy riding the etheric highways.

Then, the buzzing, a cricket's grating and chirping whine, the noise of a room full of thousands of anguished cicadas, crop destroying locusts, deafens and fills my ears, my head, whites out anything that would make sense, rhyme or reason.

Crying. Eyes hiding, face palmed, head tilted, weeping willow body hanging forward in grief. The pregnant with pain sadness, the body shaking sobs. The earth quaking, insides breaking, heart emptying keening.

There is an empty, black hole in my center where the pain mostly lived. It is sore and tender, bruised and ragged. Jagged. This will scar. Or heal. Cracked open. Broken.

Suriyya Begum
Nadia Iqbal

I think about Naniji a lot.

My mother often tells me that I am her curse. She said that my Naniji, her mother, used to tell her, "I hope one day you have a daughter like you." I have two sisters, but my mother says I am that daughter. My mother often tells me, I hope one day you have a daughter like you.

I think about Naniji a lot.

The three of us, we are all stubborn and sassy and mouthy and bossy. When we're mad, we always let the people around us know and we always inform them of the source of our anger, even if it's very silly. I remember once Naniji yelled at Nanaji that he bought too many potatoes.

I think about Naniji a lot.

Naniji always exuded warmth. She always wore shalwar kamiz. Her hair was always braided. She always wore a dupatta lightly covering her head. She was darker skinned than anyone else in my family.

I think about Naniji a lot.

Naniji always had my back. When I was visiting Pakistan at 11 years old, one of the neighborhood boys had called me moti, or fat. I got upset. I told Naniji. So, Naniji took me to the boy's house and yelled at him and his father.

I think about Naniji a lot.

When I was 17, I hadn't cut my hair in years. It was really long and I wanted to chop it off. My dad told me that if I wanted to get it cut then I would have to get Naniji's permission. I wrote a note in English and asked Naniji to sign it. She obliged. She signed it Surriya Begum. It was the only time I'd seen her write anything in English. It was the first time I knew her name.

I think about Naniji a lot.

Naniji lived in Lahore with Nanaji and their son and his wife and kids. She has always been in Pakistan, and only in Pakistan. I have spent most of my life in the United States. I can count the number of times that I have visited Pakistan that I can remember. When I was 5. When I was 11. When I was 14. When I was 17. When I was 19. When I was 22. When I was 25. Each visit was 2 to 4 weeks. That is, out of my 28 years of existence, I have spent, at most, 7 months of it with my family in Pakistan. That 7 months is definitely an overestimate.

I think about Naniji a lot.

When I was 11, I fought with my mother about going with her to Pakistan. When I was 14, I fought with my mother about going with her to Pakistan. When I was 17, I fought with my mother about going with her to Pakistan.

The summer between my first and second year of college, I was frolicking around my parents' house in Buffalo, when my mother, in the midst of washing dishes, looked at me, her eyes somewhat squinting, her lips flattened into a pained expression. She said, "You know my mother has breast cancer?" I shook my head, no. "Api was supposed to tell you. Why didn't she tell you?" Then, I was upset, both about the content of the information and its delivery. So, I listened to Bruce Springsteen's Radio Nowhere over and over and over again. And I cried. And I cried. And I cried.

I think about Naniji a lot.

My mother decided that she would go to Pakistan that August. Since I wouldn't be starting classes again until the end of September, she wanted me to go with her. None of my other three siblings could go. I was excited, but then I got upset with my mother about something. I told her that I didn't want to go to Pakistan with her. She told me she didn't think it was very nice for me to punish Naniji for an argument that we had. It wasn't nice.

I think about Naniji a lot.

While we were in Pakistan, Naniji had a mastectomy. My mom and my khala, my mother's sister, helped to take care of Naniji. I chilled with my family. My dad came so that when I went back, I wouldn't be by myself and so my mom could stay in Pakistan. My dad said he would buy a new television for the house. Naniji insisted that he get a Panasonic. She just felt like it was a good brand because it was the brand she'd had before.

I think about Naniji a lot.

A few weeks into my sophomore year at Caltech, I had missed a bunch of calls from my sister and my dad. I called my sister. She said, "Um, Naniji died." No preface. No afterword. Again, I was upset, both at the content of the information and the delivery. That night, I called my mother who was in Pakistan. She was very very upset. I talked to my cousin, Moshayyadda. She was stonily tacit. Naniji had not died from the cancer. She had died from a blood clot. When the doctors in the hospital in Pakistan had begun to administer chemotherapy, they had seemingly not taken into account her diabetes. The resulting complication is what killed her.

The next day, it was back to Quantum and differential equations and Organic Chemistry. Mourning and grief were very limited for me. The life my parents had created for us had kept us bound to the United States. I had spent most of my life in the United States. She had always been in Pakistan. I could not feel her absence.

I think about Naniji a lot.

Naniji was the only one of my four grandparents who spoke no English. My dad's parents had lived in England for a few decades. Soon after Naniji and Nanaji had gotten married, Nanaji went to Australia to complete his Ph.D. in Physics, leaving Naniji to care for my mother and her brother on her own. When my parents got married, Naniji encouraged my mother to go with my father to America because otherwise, it would have been really hard.

I think about Naniji a lot.

Naniji spoke Urdu and Punjabi. My knowledge of Urdu and Punjabi has always been limited mostly because my father speaks only English. Sometimes, I would try to tell Naniji stories in Urdu or Punjabi. And then she would turn to my mother and ask her what I said. I would be crushed. At least I had tried. With everyone else in my family, I could try to communicate in Urdu or Punjabi, but I would easily revert to English after any hint of difficulty. The oppressiveness of English is perpetuated with such ease.

To me, Naniji seemed like the last living relative who was untainted by colonialism. She was the purest example of Pakistaniness.

In order to really make it in America, in England, in Australia, in order to find success, in order to escape the scars of partition and British colonialism, you need to be fluent in English.

But, you know, sometimes I don't really want to make it in America.

Sometimes, I just want to be like Naniji.

Mother
Sherry L Jonckheere

You are an anvil to me.
Weighing me down with brute force.

Sinking my emotional landscape
To the depths of a frozen darkness.

I feel everything
But can't express a single word
For fear of reprisal and condemnation.

My world is stark and cold.

Sparks of fire extinguished
With every disappointed inflection,
Every judgement,
Every broken promise,
Every loss of hope.

Your toxic teaching has left me empty.
A sinking human shell

With only your anvil called "love" to hold on to.
Even at the bottom of this dark abyss
Letting go would set me free
But then leave me with nothing.

Another no-win situation,
To match my lifetime with you.

The Chapel of Dis-Enlightenment (A journey in the dark)

Cari Greywolf

Offering her shadow up to the altar of light,
eyes downcast in regret, stewed in remorse,
bitterness escaping through her lonely sighs.

Connections from the dark side gripping
a metaphorically bloodless heart,
cold and quiet; the thump, thump, thumping
stilled by grief. The multitude of little losses
had become the shroud she wore, hugging tightly
against her torso 'til there was no separation
from the underlying skin and muscle fiber.

Purity an illusion; the realization crushing.
Sinking into a puddle of self, bones become mush.
Now, without form, structure or meaning,
all her efforts seeking illumination futile.
Abandoned to embrace the depths of hell
in last moments too sharp to inhale,
too brutal for the soft tissue and spirit
of her tenuous human body to endure.

Praying for silence, looking up, blinded,
not by light, but by darkness, wraithlike,
swirling, consuming all she thought she was.
Once devoured, the ouroboros rises again,
in Sisyphean effort, grasping for light—
another doomed attempt—just out of reach.

Possibilities intrigue her as memories of
prior endeavors are kept hidden, again.

The altar of light teases, tempts, draws near
and then wantonly discards the seeker
to hug the cold, damp pavement alone,
enshrined as a sacrifice to the godless
and the gods themselves, impotent
in their temples of hope and despair
from whence lies, all lies spring forth
and flow into our cavernous illusions
of meaning, value, and pretense.

Sweeter Than Honey?
Julia W. Prentice

Do not like honey
Vanilla-dripping sweetness
The rushing high
Of too much sugar
Candy coated platitudes
Wrapped in colored icing
So pretty to the palate
For me so trite and nauseating
Choose instead the raw
The bitter brew
Naked coffee grounds
Biting edge of
Canker sore
Salt in wound
No upturned mouth
Just grimace and gulp
Devour the fatty lies
And spewed-out vitriol
Or drown in
Deepest dark depression
Choked down Oolong tea
Black pepper, pungent
Sprinkled on every feast
Drab gray, greasy, oily
Cold gravy, rancid writings
Or words that rip
Scald the throat
Like acid bile
Pucker mouths
Suck out tart juice
And leave behind
The shriveled rind

Now dry as dust;
These jagged scribbles
Like shards of glass
Swallowed whole
They shriek
A howl of famine
Or feast of meaning
They are the ones
I can read, consume
Digest and sometimes
Regurgitate into new phrases
To fill the empty void
Inside my aching gut.

I See Her Glow Now
Maureen Kwiat Meshenberg

hatred that is slick and thick,
so quick—
its own sociopathic anticipation,
how it moves through generations—
labeling us as colors,
that blend into our skin—
we are who we are within,
the power behind such sin—
more than sin,
it is a venomous poison—
hideous power that strikes,
to bite,
to kill,
it weighs on my soul—
it crushes me from the inside out,
I cry out why,
as the disturbing stories scream—
across our sky,
what becomes the worse of us—
breaks my heart bleeding,
my soul bends to listen—
to the voice of the dying,
body to bone—
how hearts can be turned to stone,
and learn to despise.
the tender beauty,
you were,
crushing your will,
your spirit,
you as woman,
you as wisdom,
you as human,

you as loved…
as you started your journey seeking,
but wait!
stop speaking,
stop breathing,
stop being.
your spirit is still alive,
it rises with the winds of change—
vindication and justice rises with you,
the solidarity of truth—
we will not bruise,
break,
go back,
to the way it was—
what hides lurking,
to begin again—
such evil will not win,
find hope with our spirit within.
she is now a star,
shining on us,
holding peace upon us,
I see her glow now—
as I weep.

Poet's note: Written in memory of Sandra Bland who died in police custody, July 13, 2015.

La Luna in Every Stage

Olivia Delgado

When your earth shakes,
Uncover fortunes from steady ground.

 The Color of Awakening

It was a conjuring,
Like an old wives tale spun in the history of southwest fauna.
Heavenly hopes sent by way of silken cactus flowers, dipped in milky cream and yellow.
Only in the night did they show.
As if they feared the weight of heat, the light from day.

Every time I passed them planted between homes,
I'd catch how the alignment of moon shined against their petals.
Twilight and tears laying to rest at their feet.

In one A.M. hues they found their voice.
And I thought, my…
Those sparks could blind the tremble.

 Tin Bird

You never know what will save you on certain days. The tradition of falling doesn't scar as much anymore, but the unraveling of it all has become lengthier with the closing of day and welcoming of moon. I can't find who I was before and after. Before nights spoke in metal and blue, before I attempted to translate allegories, before there was a there and here, before skipped stone dips and rises decorated my waist, before geography cut divides, before I tried understanding men who didn't understand themselves, before family broke, before I broke (me). It's the same with everything, this weighted trajectory.

After nights that leave ripples, after words are born to frame, after the after is too far gone to go back and there is nothing to meet such ache.

❊ *Storms like Seeds*

There will be days you'll want to name your storms. Every mystery that's knocked your breath sideways. Wondering why some deliver like saints in the end and others give such unrest. Weary of which aren't safe to consume, wanting only those that nourish. It wouldn't be life if things weren't coming apart. Paperback days of lessons pressed between seams and pages for each year like a manual on how to survive the wilderness.

❊ *Generations*

No wonder we clutch near our hearts so tight.
Palm against beat.
Faith in dark.

My Life as I Know It at Ten Years Old
Carmel Breathnach

I open the door to Mam and Dad's bedroom, slowly, carefully, trying not to make a sound. With my feet firmly planted in the hallway, I peer around the door and watch as Mam stirs in the bed.

"Hi Pet!" she manages.

"Hi Mam!"

I move into the room and head straight for the desk positioned by the wall on my dad's side of the bed. This desk wasn't always here. But now that it is, and now that Mam is so sick she rarely gets out of bed; I use it most days as my homework station. I place my English book on the table, opening it to the page my teacher instructed us to read. I was given extra homework today for talking too much in class. It will take me hours to get through it all. Mam lets out a loud sigh. I turn in my chair.

"Are you…?"

But she's asleep. I turn back to my book. I wonder how her day was. Was it a bad day for her? Dad will be home from school soon and my brother also. Sr. Joan is in the kitchen, watering Mam's sprouts. I want to be here, close to Mam.

Sr. Joan knocks lightly on the door and steps into the room. Mam wakes.

"Hello, Sr. Joan!" she manages.

"Ah Kathleen, are you doing alright, love?" She moves over to Mam's side. I turn back to my reading while she helps Mam with something and I wonder if I could have done whatever it is Sr. Joan is doing for my mother. Sr. Joan says she'll see us in a few days and leaves the room quietly.

"Will I read you something, Mam?" I whisper.

"Okay, Carmel!"

I pick up my book and walk around to her side of the bed. Mam's eyes, once so full of life, so warm and loving, stare at me blankly—her ten year old daughter—her angel. For a moment, my voice catches in my throat though I've seen this blank stare before. Mam has been sick for years now, and recently things are getting much worse. She is so thin she appears skeletal; her frame helpless on the bed, the vibrant and happy mother I once knew no longer here. I read and Mam's eyes close. I'm not sure what to do, whether or not to go on reading. I don't think there's any point. Mam's breathing is soft and steady in her sleep. I stare at her and I want to hug her, want to kiss her cheek but it's so hollowed out now. I go back over to the writing desk and sit down.

I think about my school day and how I got in trouble again for talking to my friend. Teacher says I talk too much and now I have extra homework. I'll do it, as I always do, but I'd prefer to stay home from school tomorrow and sit with Mam, even if she is asleep.

Grief's Love
Carolyn Riker

Grief's love is transparency
the shudder of silent loss
a scrape of thorn against paint
shuttered eyes locked
with pine barren thoughts;
I walk with shadow's trees
shoreline drawn erratic
for grief's love escapes
from lips cracked
of aged memories
and dream, may I,
on a Heron's wingspan
to current safety
nary, nonetheless the whole
essence of grief's love.

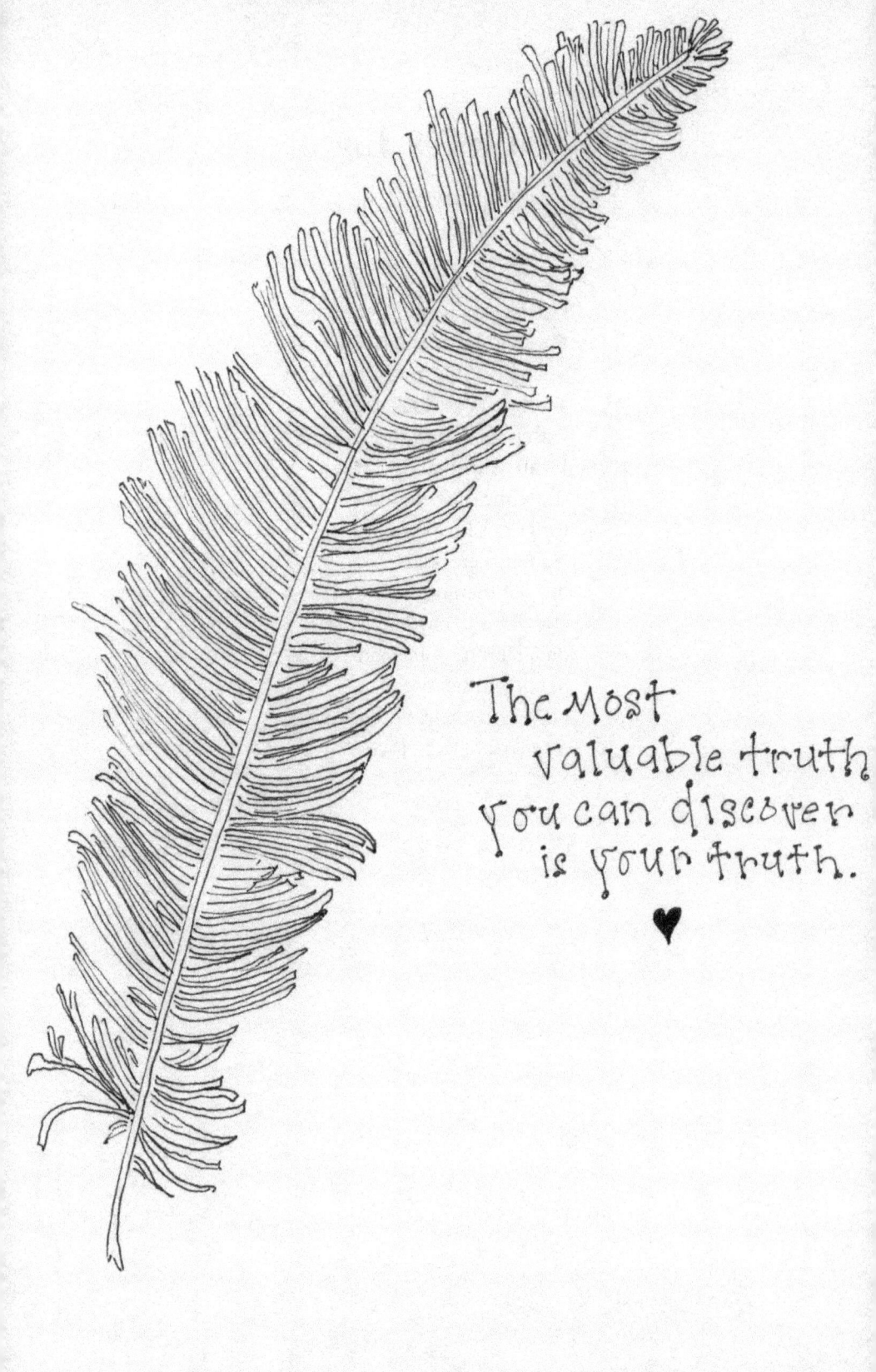

CHAPTER 3

I AM WORTHY

*"Start now. Start where you are. Start with fear.
Start with pain. Start with doubt. Start with hands shaking.
Start with voice trembling but start. Start and don't stop.
Start where you are, with what you have.
Just…start."*

—Ijeoma Umebinyuo

I Claim My Space

Jennifer Jepson

I have been learning to stand my ground and hold my space.

When the well-known voice of self-criticism and doubt tries to keep me from expressing myself, I can kindly and warmly thank that part of me. I can now breathe and land deep into my being, and approach that feeling of unworthiness and fear with kindness and love.

When faced with the fear of stating my opinion without apologizing, I can tell that part that not only am I an adult, but I am a woman. I am a woman and like my mother and grandmother, and all the women before them, I am strong to the core.

I don't have to appease. I don't have to hide. I do not have to argue, and I do not have to agree. I don't have to smile, and I don't have to pretend.

I trust my intuition and I trust my experience.

I can say how I feel with a firm quiet resolve. I do not have to people please. I do not have to prove myself. All I have to do is be me. I claim my inherent worth.

I claim my space.

Keep on Keeping
Annie Dear

Lifting the rocks
of my life
I look for joy
and searching
seemingly in vain
I wonder where it can be
hiding
'Choose joy'
says the wisdom
prevailing
but how can I choose
what isn't there?
Moments of joy
slip in through my window
with the music and the sun
and the trees and the clouds
and embrace me
in the hugs and smiles
of my loves
But when I lift the rocks
of my life
and look for joy
the sadness seeps out
And I weep
for the child whose
joy was drained
by careless love
and harsh words
and shaming silence
—never golden at all
 And I resolve to keep
loving and looking

and grieving
and receiving
until one day
bubbling over the rocks
of my life
the joy will flow back
and find me.

Away From the Sun
India R. Adams

Away from the sun and in the shadows
Is how it feels when I'm awake
My body says I am young
My heart and soul say I am not what the mirror reflects
I can feel the depths of my ancient ways
as I cling to the walls that contain me

I shiver as my world trembles
the violent ones who profess to know the truth
consume the air I need for life
A flash of despair
A moment of hope
These are the things I hold on to
Things that won't let me shatter into pieces

Away from the sun I close my eyes
and release myself into the unknown.

The Beloved Within
Lauren Love

Sometimes *dis-ease* within the body can arise to call us deeper into ourselves, to signal where we have unresolved emotions and deep healing that we have pushed under the carpet. Sometimes it takes the body becoming sick or imbalanced to wake us up to our own love, to the beauty and sacredness of our body, and to fall deeply in love with ourselves.

This was written in the women's outpatients' waiting room when contemplating the fate of my cervix.

She dropped deep into her body and felt into her cervix for the first time. Waves of grief began to arise within her, for all the times she had denied herself, for all the times she had shamed herself, for all the moments where she had allowed herself to be used and abused. She felt raw and vulnerable—ashamed to be Her. Ashamed to be inside this earthly body. She felt dirty, yucky and regretful that she had allowed herself to become so disconnected from her body, to allow herself to behave and be treated as she had done. Times of the past reverberated within her cells, a dreaded sense of shame flooded her body.

In this moment, she realized that it was time to sink even deeper into her body, to stop running from herself and to own and honor all that she is and all that she has been up until this moment. *Shame isn't who she is. Dirty isn't who she is.*

She is a beautiful young woman who made unhealthy choices. She can now have compassion for her younger self and see that she was just longing to be loved. That she allowed herself to be promiscuous and sleep with men who didn't love her, who didn't respect her and didn't care for her, because she was yearning for the closeness that she never received from her Father.

She was crying out for love and affection, yet seeking it in all the wrong places. In a culture where we are taught that sexy is desirable, that sex is in higher regard than love, and that to be wanted is the ultimate goal of woman, she had followed the familiar shadows of a destructive path... leading into the abyss of self-destruction.

Little did she know all she had to do was venture into her own heart, into the horizon of love that had always been sprawled across her chest. Only she held the key to the love that she had been seeking. It just took being present with herself and facing her own body with the deepest compassion that allowed the key to be turned. Slowly unlocking the door to her own heart...

Returning home to the Beloved that had never left her.

Ordinary Sees Extraordinary
Carolyn Riker

Whiplashed heart
crushed to bare glass blue
weary,
to bone's core
key strokes still fused
with virtual inkblot stares
surreal, is the feel
of feathery parchment
She crafts it to safe sailboat size
and voyages inner tempest
of why
and sees
ordinary people
share their
extraordinary stories
and cries
a deep sea blue.

Goddess Incarnate
Shilo Quetchenbach

They sling words like weapons to bind you, blind you;
They teach young girls to be pretty, beautiful, proper,
Pure and innocent, empty of rational thought,
The easier to control them—control you,
The easier to break your spirit,
      And you—
You, who no one told to be pretty and not smart,
(Or, if you were, you never felt their message strike true)
Did their words fail to reach their target?
Or did you, with your indifference, shrug them off?
Pretty was for other girls—shallow, shadow, defeated girls,
      And yet—
Did they sting, those barbed words that slipped beneath your defense?
The ones that said you were never—could never be—enough?
Pretty enough, proper enough, thin enough,
Beautiful enough, feminine enough…
      Enough!
Did you reject merely the notion of beauty, or of womanhood entire?
      And yet—
Were all those crushes on girls real if you didn't admit them?
(Not even to yourself)
Was it your pregnant body that you hated?
Or their decree that you must, unquestioning, feel only love?
Was it the extra pounds that dragged so heavy on your soul?

Or the weight of society's expectations?
Were you any less a goddess because the worship of your body as a vessel left you cold?
      And yet —
Was it the trappings, the wrappings, the suffocating lies that you rejected?
Or was it merely that they were forced upon you, all unasked?
      The truth is —

You will never fit into society's broken mold;
You are too bright, too bold, too beautiful,
Stronger than spider silk, a mother's love, tempered steel,
More radiant than the sun.
    The truth is —
Give them your pity,
Those dull shadows, already broken,
That try to break your spirit just to give themselves one moment,
One glittering instant to remember:
They were goddesses, once, too.
(But they could never shine as bright as you)
    The truth is —
You are not alone in this;
You can smile, laugh, and defy their labels,
Root yourself into the ground,
Stretch your arms up to the heavens,
And there, bridging the two, let your spirit fly free.
    The truth is —
When the ground shakes with the force of your conviction,
Your roots will hold fast,
While the shackles they try to bind you with fall broken at your feet.
    The truth is —
You are not alone;
You are a goddess incarnate,
And you are loved.

The Bear's Savaging
Nancy Shiner

It is cold on the stairs. Bone-chilling cold. The kind of cold that seeps beneath your skin and wraps itself around your lungs and squeezes until you can no longer breathe.

Breathe my child…breathe. But breathing is no longer an option.

She sits in the dark of a stairwell shaft, school basement below and house above, a purgatory between two Hells, because Heaven doesn't exist in this place. The cement beneath her thinly-clad shorts is hard and rough, unyielding in its assertion that there will be no comfort to be had here. No pity for the weak, even if the "weak" is a three-year-old child, hunched in the dark on cement stairs that will once again steal her innocence—if innocence can be stolen from a child that never knew innocence in the first place.

A cherubic face with a serious look, old, tired soul beneath blonde wispy pigtails, pink plastic barrettes. Tiny bare knees drawn up to her chin, little arms clasped around her shins, shoulders shaking, head bowed.

Become numb my child. Become numb.

She is afraid of the dark. Scared of monsters and ghouls and things that go bump in the night. Because she more than most knows that monsters are real and ghouls do exist beneath even the smiles of the mildest of men.

And as beam of light from the doorway above captures portrait of fate in frozen stance, its light throws shadow, a ghost of a warning, she sits and she waits in silence aware.

"The bear is coming!" her mind wails in terror. "He's coming to get me!" she cries from within. Then shadow descends, bear lumbers towards her, throat chokes with horror, walls start to dim. Prey to his predator, lamb to his lion, child-body carrion, mauled by the bear.

Mind sees "bear" as the beast, yet crime just as real, spirit bloodied and beaten, child forced to submit. This child taught from birth to keep secrets and tales, knows that men don't eat children, thus must be a bear. And with pondering question, beasts two-legged, four? Tolerance spent, she splits from within.

She sets herself free from the madness surrounding, cleaves body from soul to flee horrors that chase. And though body still huddles in darkness enslaved, she throws mind to the wind to save sanity's face.

But the truth of the picture is never so simple; fairy-tales end with beasts captured and killed. Yet for this damaged child no such fairy-tale ending, still trapped on those stairs an eternity since. Locked in darkness within a four-decades-old body, with voice that could scare even bears from their hunt. Yet child remains mute, adult-tongue long since silenced, a legend of secrets masks pain never ceased. Thus body still locked on that stairway to Hell, her mind long since fled to the dark corners four, to observe from safe distance her ongoing death in the maw of a bear who continues to feast.

A Life Called Survival
Mariann Martland

i didn't ask to be taken like that, all young,
innocent and easily-broken into any mold of life they offered
or insisted upon. i never wanted to be shaped

into the easy play-thing for their desire. i didn't change
to make life harder for you,
i was merely existing in a life as close to death
as one could possibly be; a life called survival,
not living, never living.

and yet i know (i always knew)
i was not made to survive.
i am here for something more, or less, but never
to fit this box named 'survivor' that i could neither bear nor fit. and
so i changed. i made myself
less moldable to their each and every whim, but

i didn't ask to find myself on the outside looking in, to a life
filled with shadows; screaming to be heard and killing myself
to be seen. i never wanted to change your world
with my honest word.
i just wanted you to love me.

My Mother has a Mirror
Judi Lenehan

My mother has a mirror
It amplifies every
Imperfection
Distorting
Everything that we see
It keeps us focused on flaws
And limits our direction
Nose, eyes, sallow skin
Absolutely no chance
At
Perfection
Small and square
Such a narrow
Reflection
Drifting and blurring
Never occurring
This life
Lost, and
Hurting
My father eats
Off a broken
Plate
Late
His hands rough
And his eyes
Soft
His laughter
Embraces
As it chases,
Chases the feeling
Kneeling
Slumped like a snow man

Fragile and thin
Caving, collapsing
In
I melt
Into water, water and dust
I endure, endure
And I
Rust.

Winged Dream
Olivia Delgado

There is much you can learn from howling dogs.

Reality sets in at funny times. Truth often comes clouded in mundane rituals. During the roaring symphony of barks quieting your mess of a mind.

It arrives early morning around 2 AM while watching the movie Erin Brockovich. Still believing, like you did as a young girl, that struggling women can overcome fucked up standards. Knowing that somewhere there are relationships that are built on equal faults and support.

It appears during the light of day while scouring old Bonnie Raitt songs. Considering what provoked such beautiful lyrics and how they were scribed beyond the blues.

It transpires while you're lured to the floor, because standing up is too much.

It leaves you lying in numb colors.

Most of all though realizations sneak their way in, crushing every chamber of your heart, when you least expect them.

The difficult discoveries of others hurt more than any of the ones latched to me.

For there are letters that will no longer stick to my throat…

And all I want is to remind her that women are worth more than what he expects you to be.

Remember there are gentlemen that roam this earth still.

So shelve your energy

For worthier nights

For worthier men, dear.

Cause you are a winged dream.

At the Bottom
Lisa Antley

It's cold and dark down here.
I'm steadily sinking deeper,
harder into the abyss of my own hopelessness.

Heaven help me.
Save me from myself.
I'm weak and tired.
My thoughts overcome me.
The struggle is real.
I'm at war with myself.
Nothing makes me feel good anymore.
Nobody seems to understand.
My whole world is numb,
yet I feel everything and don't want to.

Should I pop these pills,
smoke this weed or drink this liquor
To get high quicker?

Anything to escape from reality…

Even sex someone who doesn't love me and isn't worthy?

No, I'm better than that!

This is just one piece of the puzzle.
There is still more life to live—
A bigger picture to turn these negatives into positives.

The Unspeakable Act
Cari Greywolf

A young man turned thirty.
His work family surprised him:
a party to mark the milestone.
He smiled, convincingly said thank you.
Clients greeted him with congratulations.
Who knew of the weight
he bore inside that day,
what burden lead him
to end his life barely
two weeks later?

Everyone suspects, yet none are brave enough to say the word.

Suicide—
the secret,
shrouded in shame,
unspeakable to some,
held silently in our hearts.
Some things you just know.
Heaviness of denial fills his office.
The lights cast dark shadows of grief.
Words unsaid, heads nod, eyes avoided.
The once cheerful hello choked back,
heavy hearts dam the cascade of tears.

A young man will never see thirty-one years.

Someone needs to say the word,
break the spell of pretense,
make his death a visceral reality
instead of this dull, gray haunting.
A young man just turned thirty now lies dead.

His body waits to be lowered into
the ready, gaping hole in the earth
where gay or straight no longer matter.
His was a sensitive soul—
one which could not bear the weight of his truth.
Nothing is normal in the world today.

Grounded

Mariann Martland

The floor has fallen out from under me more times than I can recall. I have hit rock bottom and found it goes deeper still. Deeper I have plummeted, deeper and deeper. I have drowned and died again and again, sinking to the depths of the ocean's bed which holds only the discarded and unfound. Still, I find myself buried alone.

Digging myself out and picking myself up often feels like an inevitable falling, back to the ground that breaks my bones and shrouds me in darkness. And now, I have nothing left to climb with; the body is weary, tainted, damaged and my rope has unraveled, snapped, frayed.

But here, in this burning core in my pit of despair, there is no safety granted, much less guaranteed. Living here is no option. I must rise or sink deeper into this crumbling, breaking resting place they call hell (and home).

Yet there are times when I find comfort here. I have fallen to my bruised knees under the deafening sounds of visceral sobs and been held by the dirt. I have curled my body into the rocks, for their bed felt softer than the knives which grew from my pillow.

I have hidden under mud and matter to shield the eyes of the world. Tunnels have been hollowed and trenches built, removing sludge and slime to find refuge from the strangers' gaze and the hands of the ones who know.

I have rested on razor-sharp roads to receive momentary glimpses of stars that move quickly into the distance. Gravity has grabbed me, pulling me back to grit and gravel, as my mind wandered into lands of danger and horror of a past unfolding.

Then, my roots destructed with the foundations I was built upon. I have broken ground; a ground created through generations of lies that lived unharmed until they consumed and crushed my fragile life, but with them I crashed and exploded, detonating with a force so great that even this ancestral structure could no longer be born upon.

I have shaken the earth on which I stand, forcing secrets to scream. I have caused earthquakes through histories, revealing terrifying truths and breaking toxic ties. Craters of damnation have pushed holes through my body, allowing momentary sightings into my soul, giving more reason to look away from the bloody mess on show.

There are sometimes those who remain solid, steadfast with their presence, offering vacation holdings to rest my heart upon.

And then there are those who run to idyllic hidings where I become a less and less welcome visitor, with whom I find that even their candy-floss carpets cannot hold me home.

We are Worthy
Carolyn Riker

"I tore myself away from the safe comfort of certainties through my love for truth—and truth rewarded me."—Simone de Beauvoir

I settled lightly on the edge of a dream and began to soar. Between closed eyes the terrain became waves upon a golden shore. Mammoth ethereal wings brushed my skin and I was lifted high above to see a timeline sketched in the sand dunes of my mind.

The past was a devastating richness of mishaps, heart-crushing lessons, experiences and the vitality of surviving. It's all laced with opportunities to transform the mundane and exceptional and tragic into the purpose of gifts to be shared.

The alchemy has been happening all along. Our metamorphosis takes on different shapes.

It is as necessary to lay with heavy wet mulch as it is to rise and risk and expand and fly. Change is always happening even when we are stuck and where edges are conflicted and nothing seemingly makes sense. Somehow though, people believe in us and we begin to recognize our own unique empowerment; it embraces the purpose of heart.

We step into the now and not the never. We uphold an inner trilogy of:

We are worthy. We are loved. We are powerful.

And this is the part that really grabs a few dozen tissues from an endless zenith of heart:

We are capable to do anything.

Poet's note: Originally published in *Blue Clouds*.

CHAPTER 4

I AM SEEN

*"When we speak we are afraid our words
will not be heard or welcomed.
But when we are silent, we are still afraid.
So it is better to speak."*

—Audre Lorde

Upper Mind Strength
Jody Kristine Johnson

I am a thousand pounds of sensitivity
feeling emotional depths
in technicolor
and prone to painting
my anxiety all over the wall.
Very few can balance my weight
with grace
their arms bow with the strain
of my agonizing.
It takes resilience
and massive inner strength
to hold me
to hear me
to feel me without fleeing
and those
who have accomplished this
have the mental chests
of champions;
the ability to move
mountains.

Eggshell Stomping
Annie Dear

lately
I've been practising
eggshell stomping
and I think my toes
are a little bruised
and scratched
and tender
from walking firmly
through
the unaccustomed
remains
and I long to step
back and safeguard
my delicately
fearful toes
but I won't
those eggshells
needed breaking
they were trapping
my heart
and yours
and I'm going to keep on
keeping on
until all the fear is gone
and eggshell stomping
becomes my norm
and I respond to you
and your eggshells
with love
only love.

Unsolicited Advice
Marianne Pownall

I think it's very important that people are able to distinguish between a 'victim mentality' and post-traumatic stress which becomes trapped in the body after traumatic experiences. This is not something that we can simply talk ourselves out of. It's not 'mind over matter', as appealing as that idea is. We cannot discipline ourselves out of trauma or just give ourselves a pep-talk.

Post-traumatic stress disrupts and changes the physiological state of the body and makes it harder, if not practically impossible, to function in a 'normal' way in the world, and it isn't something that necessarily just heals itself over time, certainly not without the right circumstances and often not without the right professional support.

This is another reason why I believe it is not useful, and in fact detrimental, to separate the body and the mind, because finding true healing after trauma often means going into the body.

The right healing can also be incredibly difficult to find and often trauma can be chronically maintained by ongoing stress that is either the same stress that caused the original trauma (for example, domestic abuse) or other day to day stresses (such as bullying at school or in the workplace) which prevent the initial trauma from healing. People are not weak or wallowing in victimhood if they haven't been able to access the correct support or to change their situation.

Trauma in the body could set a person up with what others might describe as a victim mentality. Victim mentality is basically a state of disempowerment when a person does not feel in control of one's life situation. Therefore the emotions and the mind-body signals may encompass feelings of self-pity, despair or a lack of resilience in certain situations. Blame is not useful here, but compassion is. Compassion heals, whereas blame and judgment only provoke either defensiveness, shame or both, and ultimately these feelings just entrench patterns further.

Whether the blame and judgment are coming from within or from without (from our own inner critic or from the criticism of others) they are debilitating. Blame and judgment may sometimes inspire a 'positive' short-term reaction of obedience bred out of fear but they are not ways to create sustainable change.

Offering unsolicited advice can also often provoke defensiveness, whereas listening without judgment and demonstrating compassion can create catharsis, allowing the body mind to relax and initiating the internal healing process.

Sustainable change comes about through listening with love and compassion, not through blame and judgment.

Maybe through trying to change the way we communicate with one another, we can truly change the world. Maybe we can begin by first learning to observe how we communicate with ourselves. Maybe then we can start to bring that level of compassionate awareness to all of our interactions. Maybe, at this point in time, one of the most vital things we can do is to develop a sensitivity and awareness to how our internal language and our speech impact ourselves, others and consequently the earth we are trying to live on together, healthily and happily, the earth whose stewards we are, who so desperately needs us to start working together to protect her.

I don't believe we are here to clamber over one another to try and reach the 'top'. I don't believe we are here to compete. I don't believe we are here to perpetuate false hierarchies under which we have lived for thousands of years. I believe we could instead, find a new way, a way of cultivating ever greater levels of love and compassion for ourselves, one another and the earth we live on, and in doing so, we could change everything.

Disappearance & Other Acts of Magic

Shannon Crossman

Depression is a bit like being a chalk outline of a human. The outside edges are all there, but the insides have gone missing. Scooped out of the place where life should be burning and vibrant. An outline can't get far, missing a heart, organs, muscles, bones, and other structures that make motion possible.

In this place, I lose track of myself. I forget to shower for days. Until the sour, familiar stink of my own sweat penetrates my nostrils, momentarily returning small bits of consciousness. I've lived here for weeks, months, collectively years of my life.

Hollowed out. Inert inside. Listening to the dark whispers of my mother's voice ricocheting off the inside of my skull, "No one is ever going to love you. You're never going to amount to anything. You're stupid. Fat. Ugly."

The lexicon of my childhood recorded on the backs of synapses and etched into the tissue of a brain. Words that when I am bumped —just the right way—begin to play in an endlessly repeating loop. Litanies lacquered in place by childhood innocence that gobbled up every poisoned spoonful she offered. *I didn't know better, couldn't have rejected the extended bite even if I wanted to.*

I'm glad I am not there now. Grateful I've relocated my innards. Again. Put my heart back inside its thoracic cage. Strung my intestines like Christmas tinsel around the cavity of my abdomen. Reformed every muscle. Replaced each bone just so. Packed the monster voices back in the crate. Wrapped it in chains. Padlocked it and stuffed it in some sub-basement in my psyche.

Most days, I prayed for the artistry of a magician's small power to make things vanish. Only recently did I realize I already possessed the skills I sought. *I'd just been applying them in the wrong direction—*

disappearing me instead of the remnants of maternal disdain that clung to me.

Now, as I come to realize my error, I know that someday soon I shall reverse the tide. Next time I raise my wand, whisper the incantation, "be no more." I can assure you I won't be directing the spell at myself. No. Finally, I'll turn the wand around and zap that fucking crate, last remembrance of my desperate un-mothered past, right out of existence.

My Writing Room

Nancy Shiner

I step into my writing room, tablet clutched firmly in hand. With a sigh of pleasure, I sink into the warm bubbles, allowing the water to flow over my skin and lap at my chin. I have entered the temple of my sacred space where words pregnant with possibility echo against the tiled walls and drip onto the floor where they puddle to form whole paragraphs.

Perhaps the nakedness of my physical form, the vulnerability of skin exposed, requires me to enter a place of courage to reveal my naked soul with words and thoughts untethered by pulled cloth and zippered lip. As though my feelings have no choice but to mirror the vulnerability of the skin I am wearing.

My writing room?

It is the space within my body where I force the words to rise from their decay in the bowels of my soul to enter through the shameful groin of a woman long denied. Denied the right to feel and express, to birth its seeds through the pains that labour their body's release. To give them permission to flow through a belly restricted, kept hungry to avoid the gluttony of spewing forth too much, having left my words to starve before they provide the nourishment needed to keep my soul alive.

They slither up arms ringed with scars, countless bands of ruined tissue that scream of tales that must never be told. So my words fall silent and creep past quickly onto safer terrain. They crawl up my throat in the hopes of release. Surely here I will have my voice, but they choke me with their emotion. Their largeness, their tales of truth that steal my breath with their knowing.

And through the mirror of my eyes where their truth can no longer be denied, their pain finally finds its release as teardrops glide. Then stream, then cascade down weary cheeks 'til they slide off my chin to mingle with the river of countless words drowning amidst the bubbles beneath me.

The water now chilled, skin shivering from both cold and effort, my words contract with the temperature's drop.

I pull the plug.

Words swirling down the drain, I am once again empty.

Stilted
Judi Lenehan

She balances teetering on her *shoulds*
trying to lift herself on rigid poles
her feet touched into harsh stirrups

Tight and uncomfortable
they tether her to inflexibility

Drag then lift
drag then lift

The world is smaller from up here
and instead of being higher up,
seeing further into the future
she remains mesmerized
by the ground
and the prospect
of it rushing to meet her

Grinding her to a halt
Halting steps
Clicking, clacking
Others seem to do so much so effortlessly

Circus performers in contrast to her side show by the seashore
All she wanted was a decent conversation
A bit of inspiration
Not an expiration date
But fate
Twisted her forcing her thru a wire hanger
And she felt like a stranger
Lacking place
And presence.

Pelos: This Body of Mine
SK Lockhart

My youngest nuzzles
into the crook of my shoulder
breathing deeply
his fingers gently stroke
the *pelos* under my arms

mama, this is where you smell
the best, it's your
mama scent
sweet, like warm toast

his words soothe away
vestigial shame
once burned into my skin
in the shape of a paradox,
undesirable
even as uninvited hands
held me down

this body,
loved so much by him,
grounds him
in the world,
though
sometimes
i can only see battle scars
and blotchy veins,
stretch marks, and
hanging fat

he revels in my jiggly skin
eagerly reading the marks

from pregnancy...like a favorite
story
they wrote our tale,
connect us, and
he understands
those visceral memories

i made a stand in my twenties,
to leave my body hair intact
and let my body be itself
even with eyes on me,
my mother's voice
pleading

my redemption began with
the voice of
another child
in the mountains of Guatemala
reverently
admiring the soft
pelos curling on my legs
confirming what i had suspected

and now
it is up to me
to teach my sons that
women's bodies are
real, they are strong
they bring life and write
the stories of creation.

WANT

Jaymz Hawkes

I tried to talk to you, ask you about your history, tried to connect with you on a different level, tried to ask you things, sometimes you would answer and you spoke. I would listen so intently, when you spoke.

How did you know? Did you ask someone, or did you do everything to me based on a suggestion, that, I might have been an answer or a prayer?—but no, you thought I was an error, and that I didn't want to be you. You told me your address and wanted me to be there, for your shame, became mine, because you knew I'd turn up and flood the lights, drown the memory and open the gates and cause a storm—this part you knew.

I have lost time suddenly, amidst an escape from you, doing everything to me that I never wanted—forgetting what I needed, running from what happened, and it all shaped me into, you.

It doesn't matter how many envelopes I have mistakenly opened, they all lead to you.

I am, nothing wrapped up in a surprise gathering or sweetened look and feel—I am, something, so small so insightful and yet insignificant, and I've landed here—and I've never asked why, because I'm supposed to be 'Happy'…

It is the synthesis, the snake in the grass, the sounds of forget and allow. A past glare, it already took my left eye, now I'm staring down the barrel of a gun, when I thought it was supposed to be over.

Whose hand is about to hold the trigger this time?

I'm not making any sense because there's nothing to say. And you, are not the reason or the fall. No, I can't even give you that—but it turns out, I'm just like you.

I am writing the footnote. I ask no one anymore as it's the same thing every day and it is the same shit which covers my eye—on a platter, made from my memories, which no matter what I do, it's there.

Yeah, I'm pissed off. And maybe that's why I'm nowhere.

So the dead horse has been awakened, I sit here—I can't fucking move. Nothing. And I have, everything, I wanted.

How does the mind bend into this, and why am I not here anymore. I found the keys, they were in the grass, beside the snake, the envelopes, and no surprises.

If you think I'm asking to be forgiven, think again. If you think, I care what you're doing now, you're probably right—as last night, I was walking through South Street, and it's something you wanted, so I rode my bike and bought you some cigarettes.

That was a time, I had reprieve, and I would ride my bike with no hands racing down that hill as dangerously fast as I could. The man at the shop asked me how old I was, I said, "I am Seven". He always gave me a bag of lollies and disapproved of me doing this errand for you, and wanted to report you—but I took my time, and walked home, after sitting under a tree and eating the free bag of lollies. I opened the new pack of Dunhill Red for you—because, I was late. I smelt the tar and pulled out your first cigarette and I lit it for you. This was the only time you were calm.

I tried to talk to you, ask you about your history, tried to connect with you on a different level, tried to ask you things, sometimes you would answer and you spoke. I would listen so intently, when you spoke.

I was only seven. I could see you, you didn't want me to. You hated me. You asked me to just go away. I wasn't coming undone. I wasn't confused, angry or frustrated. I wasn't afraid of you, and that all angered you.

I just wanted to know you.

Safeguard the Goodness Within
Annie Dear

and I gather the goodness
with care
and place it safely
into the little velvet bag
with the drawstrings
pulled safely shut
and I hold the bag
gently
and stroke its velvety
blackness
and savour the goodness
within
and all around me
the loss and the pain
and the lonely
emptiness
try to squeeze
past
into the velvety warmth
within
but I won't let them
and they gather me
round
and try to steal the
goodness
from my care
but safe in the black
velvety darkness
the goodness remains
and holding the bag
with care
I can feel its warmth
and soft laughing
love
and I can remain
too.

Self-Identity Slowly Rises
Don R. Johnson

The naming takes a lifetime.
Feeling and experiencing precede it.
Fear of an angry Father roars itself
in physical violence. His utter
confusion at my failure of masculinity
later gives way to respect and love.
Female protectiveness in a Mother
and in a sister of angelic mercy.

Inability of self-defense in the face
of bullying and the macho way
is more than a foreign word.
Vivid memory of presence and
sickness while male bonding
repeatedly drops concrete block
on the shell of an innocent turtle.
Voicelessness and guilt within.

Deepened in a familial sense of
imperative to learn patterns
and inhabits the growing mind.
Essence in curiosity and attentiveness.
Understanding and compassion
inform a spiritual journey outward
to the lives of others and self.
Self-identity slowly arises.

Collecting Pieces of Her
Ilda Dashi

There she is,
this mirror is showing her all her parts,
some neglected,
some denied,
some condemned,
some embraced tenderly,
in the rain of her old tears,
in the train of her dark fears,
and the tender traces of her past memories.
There she is,
nude in front of her own image,
counting all her stars painted upon her lips and eyes,
but also confronting her vulnerable wild spirit…in all its colors.
There she is,
alone with her hands on her breasts,
and her sight on the landscape of her thighs…!
Her mind begins to comment and dislike few of her corners and curves,
calling them ugly, dirty or not proper…
While her eyes tell her to believe in their beauty instead…!
There she is,
naked in her vulnerability.
Confusion…
Delusion…
Illusion…!
There she is,
trying to pick up all the pieces of herself together,
to make them one,
in order to care for herself,
to not feed further the separateness of her being,
as she once was taught…!

Nothing Was Ever Enough

SK Lockhart

Shame. fear. sadness. flashes of what a bleeding wrist would look like with blood gushing out. would it feel so hot that it actually feels icy? would it hurt or would i be so numb that it wouldn't matter? i think it is just a fantasy, but sometimes i am not entirely sure. blood is a big part of the last month. i have now been bleeding for 24 out of 27 days. it defines me lately, even when i don't want it to. it stains my visions the way it stains everything else.

regret. lots of regrets. knowing i am pushing people away. feeling convinced that it is for their own good and mine. i am the one who has nothing to offer, and i don't want them to find out for themselves. knowing how crazy that sounds, but feeling trapped anyway. stuck in a rut with no other answers. i have phone numbers to call, but i can't let them see me like this. they may disappear, and what will i do the next time, when it feels even worse? better to know that someone might be there someday than risk ruining it with neediness and chasing them away now.

watching the dying leaves fall from the trees. feeling the tears slip down my face. at least they are flowing. wishing this didn't have to be me, here, alone and crying. hearing myself lie about being fine when someone walks over to squeeze my hand. it is automatic. sure, i am fine. enjoying the trees, the sounds of the insects around me. stifling sobs when that person walks away. why do i make people guess? it is impossible for them to pass the test. i make it impossible. it shames me too much. my mother's words echo….i bring a black cloud everywhere i go. i am all about negativity. i try to chase the words away but they don't leave.

i answered her question honestly. it came pouring out as we walked the dogs. no, we are still not speaking. how dare i tell others about our family secrets. who the hell am i? i feel better in the moment, accompanied, as we walk along together. then i get in my car and drive away. and my whole body pulses in disbelief. i am compelled to apologize for breaking the rules, a traitor. i should have lied again. when i admit things out loud, i become the victim. i am weak, needy. i don't know what is real.

my religion has always told me suffering is good, the ultimate sacrifice. turn the other cheek. it is an end goal, proves your worth. body and blood. real body and blood. i don't want to be really fucked up, don't want to be the martyr. deep down i know i was fucked over. i am intelligent. i can rise above. insight is my burden.

i could feel the hatred. it was palpable. i deserved it. i was hideous. clumsy. fat. ugly. no one could love a person who was hated by their family. i found people, let them in, loved obsessively. and they moved on. they left me. i tested them and they left.

i should have fought her more when she held me down to pluck my eyebrows. i had visions of physically hurting her. i hated her, hated my aunt in that moment. i hated how they made fun of me. nothing was ever enough. i would never look right. i never made the right choices.

i got curves. i could not stop my body. people noticed. my cousin noticed. they made me sit on his lap in a crowded car. it felt good. i never said yes. i was ashamed, but it was attention. he was caressing me secretly as if i were attractive. no other teen age boy had done that, except for years ago when they forced me, in their backyard. it didn't feel good with them. but this did. i hated myself as my body betrayed me. it wasn't supposed to be like this.

i obsess over people then throw them away. she loved pointing that out. she let me know i was selfish, obsessive, annoying. sometimes, when there is too much fighting, wrestling, squealing chaos i just can't take it. i want it to stop. i want someone to hear me when i say no. i hate it. no one hears me. no one ever did. i know in my head it is different now. i know my sons are not me, when i was young. but it sounds the same. my heart pounds. but the screams….are the same. and i was betrayed by my sounds. i laughed as i screamed, so it must have been fun. they grabbed and poked and held me down, tickled me and mocked me. she stayed out of the room.

and it all crashes around me. i don't deserve any attention at all. i should not be allowed to be near people. i am a mistake. my life is a mistake. i don't know how to live a mistake.

The Treachery of Breadcrumbs
Jennifer C. Zechlin

I swallow each bite,
filled with more disgust than nutrients.
The sounds of chewing so deafeningly loud in my ears
—*Can everyone around me hear it too?*
Each morsel bleeds its shame into every cell
—fattening them with plump disregard.
Why can I not gain the upper hand?
The hand that dangles above my head clutching tools of destruction
The one that plays muscles and sinew like strings of a harp.
And why does this slow dying make me feel strangely alive?
Mirrors and scales both shouting their lies
as I follow a trail of breadcrumbs (It's always bread, isn't it?)
into demon-dark forests with rabid wolves awaiting.
My body, so fat (no, really)
but my soul feels dangerously thin
—like the skin on the back of my hands
that tears so easily with age.
There are rules to make it OK,
and if only I were stronger,
I might be able to disappear into them
and fall through the black hole
—that for now only exists in my belly—
and follow the sound of that harp to hope.

We can be no more than, or less than, who we feel called to be. ♥

CHAPTER 5

LOVE IS LOVE

"The problem with gender is that it prescribes how we should be rather than recognizing how we are. Imagine how much happier we would be, how much freer to be our true individual selves, if we didn't have the weight of gender expectations."

—Chimamanda Ngozi Adichie

Jessica's Story

Jessica Wicks

My earliest memories begin around age three.

White squirrels for which Olney Illinois is famous. The lady we rented from, who lived upstairs, where I wasn't to go but she had these toys so who could resist? The little girl next door with whom I played.

Until age three, I would say I was a happy child. Until that is, one evening Mom was tucking me into bed. "That's a good little boy," she softly whispered.

"Mama, I'm a girl."

That look. A look I'd never seen before. I now know it was some combination of fear and disgust.

"You are a boy and I don't want you to ever say that again!" she shouted.

From that day forward there was a full-scale effort to man me up, and I really did try. The year was 1950. There was no name for transgender yet. Christine Jorgensen had not yet burst upon the scene. It was all sort of lumped into the category of homosexual and it was considered either illegal or mentally ill.

A year later we moved to East Texas. I look at photos of me during that time. My eyes reflect a terribly sad and lost child. In elementary school, by the third grade, the kids were first teasing, then beating me. I would hear shouts of "Queer!" and "Homo!" followed by the flurry of fists. I had no idea at that point what it meant, but I knew it must be terrible. Furthermore, my Dad assured me if I ever ran from a fight, he'd whip me worse than they ever could.

When I neared puberty, I came to understand that I was indeed both gay and transgender. In my small East Texas community, I had to build my closet well hidden away from public view. I was never able to talk with my parents about any of this. Even after Dad passed away in '67, Mom made it clear that if she ever learned I was one of 'those people'—I was no longer welcome around her.

Growing up I coped with private journals where I'd write and then burn what I'd written. I lived a quiet and lonely existence. After I grew up, I was out to one circle of friends, and closeted to another —with a sex life consisting of one night stands. In the early seventies, I tried one last time to be straight, and even married a woman who happened to be lesbian. We had one child and parted ways soon after and remained friends until our child was grown.

I could experience elements of my transgender identity through drag, but it was never really fulfilling. I hid behind alcohol and drugs as well, but they turned on me soon enough and by '84 I'd become sober, which also demanded of me critical self-examination and self-honesty. Mom died in '88 and soon after, I was preparing myself for transition. By now I lived in Houston, a safer climate for such a move.

In the midst of transition circa '90, I met Skip. This gay man, a beautiful soul with whom I was blest to find love, supported me in my journey. It was no easy journey. I lost virtually all my family. My daughter, brother, aunts, uncles, cousins, all agreed I was no longer welcome in their lives. I was yelled at, attacked, and harassed in bathrooms. Hormones also led to a shift in my attractions, now to women, but Skip and I loved each other and that did not change.

I got permission from my employer to transition on the job. I was the first ever to do it with my agency. Not everyone was on board however, and a few made every effort to sabotage my position there. Then Skip became ill and suddenly died from encephalitis. He was my first true love. In fact, he taught me what real love was. Two weeks later a dear friend passed away in my arms, a victim of a heart attack. This was truly my dark night of the soul. Yet friends and members of my support group slipped in and out of my life, and slowly I healed. What a beautiful lesson in the meaning of community.

In 1999, I met my current wife, Robin. We found love as well, though she and Skip were so different. Using a narrow court decision, we managed to obtain a same sex wedding in Texas amidst a ton of publicity. Soon after we moved to Minneapolis, where we live comfortably today.

I went from a miserable childhood to inner peace. I've a supportive church community and it has been a long time since I've encountered any in person hate. It only happened by being true to that voice of that child of three, trying to tell my Mom who I really was. I wouldn't trade my life now for the world! Society said no, but by pursuing my truth, I found that elusive happiness!

My Voice is Getting Clearer

Jhilmil Breckenridge

tell the world i am gay
tell my best friend i am lesbian
tell my mother i am queer
tell tell tell

smash patriarchy
smash patronising judgement
smash self flagellation
smash smash smash

love me, bruise me, hold me
love me, a melody on skin
love me, wild cymbals and moonlight
love love love love

liberate my indian-ness
liberate my class-ness
liberate my posh accent
liberate liberate

flaunt my hips
flaunt my tummy
flaunt own possess
flaunt flaunt flaunt

stand with my legs apart
stand and squat like i mean it
stand astride, feel earth's power
stand stand stand

my voice is getting clearer
so tell, smash, love,
liberate, flaunt, stand
clear. queer. clear. queer.

Editor's Note: Poem original published on *Gender Pages Project*: www.gender-pages.tumblr.com

Queer Enough
Shilo Quetchenbach

Do you ever feel like you don't know whether you're running away from your past or running toward yourself?

I was 30 when I found a term for my sexuality that resonated with me. When I found the courage to use it publicly. When I decided to stop hiding.

My mother told me "Oh, that's normal. Everyone feels like that," when I first tried to tell her I liked girls, too. I didn't know anyone who was queer; didn't have the language to express myself. I wrote coming-out messages to friends, only to delete them. I convinced myself that I was not queer enough.

I am happily married to a man. I have a child. And I am not straight. I never knew what the hell I was, only that I had crushes on male and female friends. That many of my favorite books featured queer characters. That even when I started quietly choosing bisexual on census forms and surveys a decade ago, it wasn't quite right.

My husband has never questioned his identity, his gender, his sexuality. I can't recall a time when I didn't. When I knew for certain anything other than that I was not straight. Not a woman. Not.

It is so limiting, defining yourself by what you are not instead of what you are. LGBT, even with the added Q+, is intimidating. Am I queer enough? I can pass. But I don't want to.

For three decades I listened to everyone who told me don't:

Don't study art. Don't reveal your mental illnesses. Don't reveal you're not normal. You'll regret it.

But it's hiding all those pieces of myself that I regret, because you can't live honestly if you're always afraid to let bits of yourself show.

I tried to mold myself into a scientist because I was smart and denied my passion for the arts. I hid my mental illnesses for fear of being thought mad. And for fear that I wasn't mad enough.

Enough. I framed my identity by what I was not, and wondered why I felt like I was never enough. Of anything.

I am tired of hiding, so here I am:

I am Queer. Panromantic Demisexual. Genderqueer. Bipolar.

I have anxiety, depression, PTSD, migraines, fibromyalgia, allergies and asthma.

I am a feminist. I am an artist and a writer.

I write fanfiction. Yes, I'm one of those people. But I'm not afraid of being thought less of, for that. Do you know why I write fanfiction?

Because through fanfiction, I've found a community. I've learned the infinitely many ways there are of being not straight. Of being yes. I've found a place to explore my identity, with all of its what-ifs and complexities.

And if I can continue doing that, it will help others find themselves too. To learn to accept those nonconforming parts of themselves—rather than telling the world all of the things I am not—instead all of the things that I am, will have been worth it.

Trans Women: A Sonnet

Margo Stebbing

No Adichie, you are not right for saying trans women grew up with
male privilege. The audacity of your words wielding such broad strokes
And with a sword severs the sisterhood to allege
giving cisgender's own privilege to invoke,

thus trans women are devalued by mainstream society on both accounts,
their overlapping oppressions as both feminine and trans
makes them the whipping girl to discount
once again not included in the wide host of feminine span.

But if we are willing to see our errors and make amends
even a feminist icon has feet of clay
be careful for trans women harm you do not intend
over half of all anti-LGBTQIA homicides are toward transgender woman, say
instead we need to include and protect our trans women more than ever
and not assume we know their experience of privilege and in that,
their safety sever.

But I'm a Man

Ryan Dumas

- Women's rights
- Feminine hygiene
- Motherhood
- Lady parts

These are things that apply to me. I have a vagina, and I have the potential to grow a child in my uterus. I need pads; I need the right to birth control, health, and abortion.

But I'm a man.

See, that causes a bit of a problem. Because I have a vagina, people assume I'm a woman. And I'm not. And while I do have some benefits from being a man (and being on testosterone for 14 months)—like not being catcalled and leered at—I still don't have basic rights.

It is legal for me to be fired, kicked out of my home, and worse. Just because I'm trans.

I am fighting to get my malfunctioning uterus out of me, but my insurance won't cover it. You want to know why? Because it could be considered a trans-related surgery.

Last time I had a period without being on hormones, I was hospitalized. It was only (yes, only) the 54th day of my period. I received two pints of blood.

And still, my insurance won't cover its removal. Because it could be considered related to my being transgender.

In case you're wondering, my record is 72 days of bleeding. Straight. Using maxi pads and the highest absorbency tampons.

Can't get the cause removed.

I have access to birth control, at least, which is more than many folks with uteruses can say.

But while I am a man, I need my rights to be fought for too.

I'm disabled and can't fight for myself. But I still need rights.

When you fight with your sisters for your rights, please don't forget about me, and the other transfolk who need these rights.

Phrasing is crucial in regards to these issues. It is a hassle. I know. But once you get used to it, it becomes second-nature. So when you are talking about people with uteruses, say that. Don't say women.

If you say women, make sure you include trans women—they are women too.

Call our parts their names. Don't call them lady parts; I'm a man, and I have those parts.

Don't call it motherhood when you're generalising. Call it parenthood.

While you're fighting for women's rights, please remember:

Not all men have penises.

Not all women have vaginas

Trans men aren't women.

Trans women aren't men.

Transfolk have very few rights.

Don't forget to fight for us, too.

TRANSSEPARATION
Jessica Wicks

I am woman. My heart, my being, my spirit and soul seeing
Screaming from every pore for all to hear…I am woman!

Touch my soul and know the vision which after body revision
Remains the same. Taste my lips a woman's lips softened by

Tears and years of caring and daring to be the same as that person
Who stares out through these weary eyes…?

So many sighs.

Tears of joy, and tears from indescribable heartbreak
Family torn asunder and former friends wonder and the loss
And hurt tearing away at ego but also taking pieces of myself along the way.

Is self-truth always this brutal? And is it so dangerous that we are killed and beaten and thrashed and trashed just for being who we are? Just the other day, two women like me, shot over and over in their car.

Is the death of transcendental souls one more symbol of the fear of a privileged gender?

Afraid to surrender even a tiny vestige of its power and hold
Over the hearts and minds and possessions of fifty-one percent of all of us?

In a world of patriarchy and privilege, I am woman.
My state says it is so, my body says it is so.
My breasts, my skin, my vagina all proclaim I am woman.
When my beloved in sensual understanding and lips and hands ever more demanding,

She brings me confirmation, and oh so erotic demonstration of love with a woman.

My essence, my energy, my dreams, loving without bounds baring my soul…

A woman's soul, complex and multilayered with dreams yet to be dared,
And hopes and loves and fears and scarred with loss untold
And yet still soft and yielding when heart touches heart

And becomes a piece of a larger universal woman centered moon empowered

Stream of consciousness that some call Goddess and others call Womyn's space

And still others do not name but are empowered just the same.

Yes I am woman and I cry like a woman and my soul feels the sheer exuberance of being just exactly who I am.

But, oh the sadness and heartbreak and heartache that comes with that word.

But…a conjunctive with repercussions in my soul and psyche that will remain always

A reminder of the price of self-truth and the consequence of being.

I turn to my closest friends, those who love me the most where trust has been so freely shared.

My friends assure me. You are so loved, so special, an energy of woman embodied.

Then the condition—'*the but*'—in my life, the anguish of the soul, the difference that separates—

Creates that chasm beyond which I cannot go.

Because of that aberration of birth, piece of unwanted undesired flesh I will always be separated. My friends say—meaning well I am sure

You are such a special person! I would love you no matter what or who you are!

No matter what or who you are? No matter what or who you are?

The words ring in my ear, a truth accepted but less desired than all other truths combined.

They clamor to explain. You are a woman, only different! I will never know first blood, or any menses for that matter. Never could I, as a child, bond with my girlfriends in the way they have done. Until I could repair the wrong that dangled below I was the recipient of privilege…

Different you know? There was no first corsage or the date who never showed. There was no father-daughter dance or first romance…
not that way anyhow.

Does it mean I am not a woman? Of course not! Just…DIFFERENT.

In a world where I was born "different" I remain now as then…
different.

Oh I love my new life and the joy and love that come from being this woman. At times makes my senses reel and my heart skip in enthusiastic glee for the woman who is me. I find the love and strength and renewing spirit of womyn's space: empowering, exhilarating, comforting, and transforming all at one time.

From one woman to another, we share our lives and our stories and our souls

And we do rituals and honor croning and maidenhood and motherhood as women have done

Throughout the expanse of life's journey. Our tears and our laughter are offered before the Great Mother, who smiles at our offerings with a gleam of delight?

But in those moments, those horrible wrenching moments when Difference rears its head, when the "But" comes to rule,

The arrow of despair pierces my heart and one more tear is offered from coffers that have no bottom.

My friends are excited! It is time for Michfest, a festival of women celebrating women.

And being women and the ultimate in what women's space is about.

A lover of women's space and women's music wishing to revel with my partner in this sacred space I become different. I am not welcome to this space. And still another tear is shed as offering to Earth Mother.

I would not understand, I could not understand. At Michigan, I am not woman, but OTHER.

So it is in my walk of life. I am woman to most, other to some, non-human to still others: Loved, hated, smiled at and reviled. Praised and hated—a source of confusion for many. I do not understand it, some say. I do not want to understand it, say others.

But life goes on and love goes on and hate and fear go on also. To all who hope that my kind will disappear and those who revel in my difference. What we have not in common rather than what we do, I smile sweetly, and offer this simple reality:

I can only be me and you can only be you and we can be we or never. But my truth will remain, agree or complain, and from my truth you cannot sever; for in truth, to self, I have found truth in others and the same for love it's clear to leave behind that which is me would leave me with nothing but fear. My soul lives, and will beyond death and it is a beautiful soul prepared to love, prepared to live, prepared to dance. If you dance with me, then we dance together, but if you cannot, I shall dance alone.

Bending Reality
Dolly Mahtani

I fought for many years so that I wouldn't fall into a label and be stereotyped because of my sexual orientation but the truth is my sexuality has completely turned my life upside down. Over and over again. It forced me to shift, to transform, to open, to fight, to be brave.

If it wasn't for my sexual awakening, I wonder what would've become of my life. Every time I try to picture it, I don't see myself alive. Sometimes I have visions of a ghost. A shadow that manages to survive but you can't really call that living can you?

My life was planned before I was even born. Since I was six years old, I knew what was expected of me growing up. I had to get good grades. I had to be kind. I had to be tidy, disciplined, obedient and girly. Always feminine. I had to learn to cook and clean because when I was old enough, I was going to be married off. I was meant to learn and love the fact that one day a man would become dependent on me to manage his home and family. That I would be swapped for dowry. This was not a maybe in my life, it was a plan. Arranged marriages were the way of my family. My mother married my father when she was just twenty years old. I listen to her story with horror.

"It was our wedding day. They had put a veil on my head but when no one was looking, I lifted it to see his face. I wanted to be able to recognize my husband," she says.

She married a man she had never seen before. A man she, therefore, did not love.

"Love is not what you think it is," they'd tell me.

"Love is like a seed. Plant it anywhere and water it so it will grow," my grandfather once told me.

It made sense to me but I couldn't fathom a marriage void of it. On top of it all, I felt the thought of being with a man repulsing. How to tell them? I couldn't. They already had a boy lined up for me. I was only eighteen at the time. Around this same time, I met her. The girl that would turn my world upside down. This actually made things a lot worse. I was paralyzed. In love with a girl in secret and engaged to a man at the same time.

In my agony, and deliberate self-pity, I came to a conclusion. I climbed to the roof of my house and stood at the edge looking down. I was so afraid of failing—to die—if I jumped. What if I ended up handicapped? What if my parents found out that I tried to kill myself? I had to make sure the attempt would be successful or not try at all. I sat on the ledge of the roof and thought about how I got here.

This was the moment of my first epiphany. I had to make a choice. A choice between happiness and duty. Love and responsibility. Freedom and obligation. I had to create a new kind of reality.

One that was not modeled for me. One where I could make decisions based solely on my heart. Where fear wasn't a subtle intruder in every experience.

Coming out to my family was the best thing I ever did. They kicked me out of the house and temporarily disowned me, of course. I thought this would kill me but it didn't.

Leaving was the second best thing I ever did. The real adventure started there. I landed in a gay-friendly country where I had no friends or family. No job or apartment. Just one big, red suitcase and an open heart. I left everything and everyone behind me. I was a blank page. I reinvented myself that day and a couple of months later I found my dream job and met my soul mate. But that's another story for another day.

The Twice-Given Gift
T.J. Banks

At the end of 7th grade, my daughter M. began talking about being bisexual. I was surprised—I'd seen no indication at that point that she was attracted to other girls—but I figured it would all sort itself out at some point.

Only some things, I was to learn, don't sort themselves out nice and neatly. Her confusion was deeper than I'd realized, and it was about a lot more than orientation. It merged with what a psychiatrist told me was "a low-grade depression" over the father she couldn't remember, creating an emotional firestorm that I was finding it hard to believe we'd ever come out of.

She cut herself, had suicidal thoughts, and once even tried to run away. There were emergency-room trips, hospitalizations, outpatient therapy, and a slow, often painful re-building of our relationship.

We got it back, though—enough so that when M. told me she thought that she was "full-on lesbian," I accepted it. After all, I had family members and friends who were gay, so it wasn't such a big adjustment. Her girlfriends came over, and we talked about what was happening in her various relationships.

But by her sophomore year of high school, there was a new bend in the road: M. had come to understand that the issue was not one orientation but of gender. That she was a male trapped in a female body. M. began dressing as a boy and calling herself/himself Zeke.

This was a harder issue for me to deal with but not for the reasons you'd think. There had been a lot of loss in my life already, and all I could think was that I was going to lose the daughter who had been my joy and comfort since Tim's death. Selfish but true.

A woman said to me, "You have been given a great gift. You had the privilege of having a daughter for many years, and now you have the privilege of having a son." She was right, of course—my brain realized that the moment she spoke. But hearts take a lot longer to catch up.

Oddly enough, it was Zeke who found the words I needed. They had been written by a father whose daughter, like mine, had realized that nature had made a mistake. "I find that I am not ready to give up the little girl that I loved so much," this unknown man had written.

"She is special to me—I love her and don't want her to go, even though I know I must. In a way, this is like a death and a birth, in the family at the same time. Allow me to mourn the loss of my daughter and, I assure you, I will rejoice at the birth of my new son."

I sat in on a support group for parents with trans children: mostly, I just listened, but it helped knowing that there were other parents wrestling with the same issues. I went to some of the counseling sessions that Zeke had with his therapist, who was transgender herself, only MTF (male-to-female) and read some of the articles she gave him. And slowly, I came to understand that the life I'd imagined for Zeke, so long ago, was not right for him.

Then came the surgeries. I went out to Arizona with him for one of them, and we stayed at a condo not far from the hospital. A couple of nights after the operation, Zeke called to me from his bedroom. Would I feel weird, he asked, checking the surgery site to see if everything looked O.K.?

I gave a mental shrug. "No," I replied. "After all, if you had been born in a male body, I would've seen it by now."

That was when my heart and I finally got where we needed to go. I had a son, and he needed looking after. Heart and I were good with that. More than good with it, really.

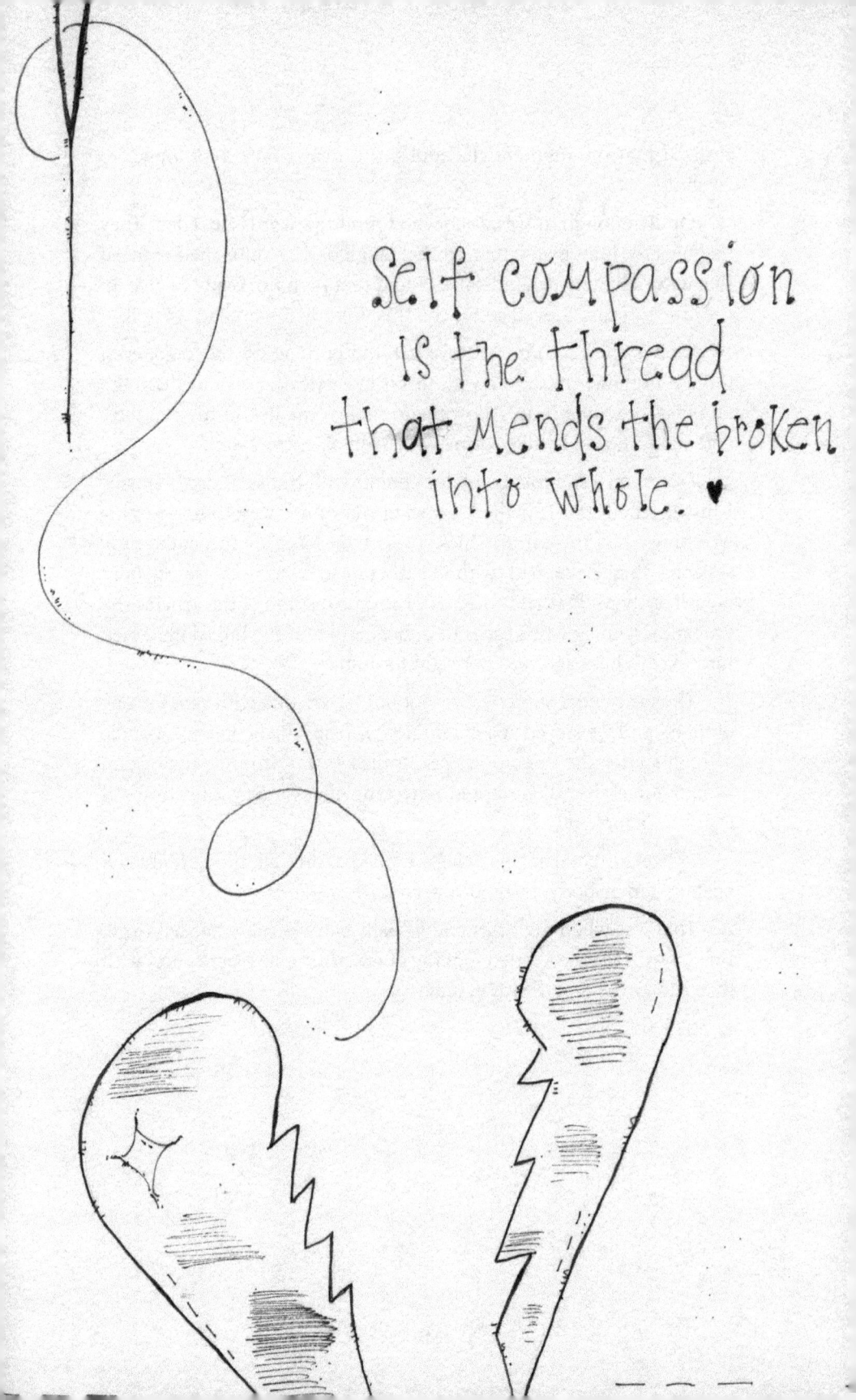

CHAPTER 6

UNSEEN SCARS

"And when at last you find someone to whom you feel you can pour out your soul, you stop in shock at the words you utter—they are so rusty, so ugly, so meaningless and feeble from being kept in the small cramped dark inside you so long."

—Sylvia Plath

Forever Asleep
Alice Maldonado Gallardo

I'm not dead.
I'm just sleeping.
Walking in my sleep
out of the hospital.
Passing sterilized corridors
of misery quarantined.
Leaving abandonment,
silently praying
silently screaming
silently disintegrating.

White feathers of a gown
escaping from this tormented body.
A body turning
into stone.
Liberation and rescue
from a frigid wheelchair.
Ripping out synthetic stitches,
holding me together,
forcing tubes to grow
out of my bones.
Purifying my blood
returning it cursed.
Examined intrusively
under glazed eyes.
Laying under a microscope,
becoming an x-ray of a soul.

Living with roommates of pain,
addicts of despair,
broken bodies suffocating

under the weight
of 100 elephants
that cannot forget.

Afraid to wake up
and find myself
still in the hospital,
unable to walk
unable to move
unable to live.

No freedom
but in my sleep.
No life
but in death.
The last moment of breath
takes forever to leave.

Poet's note: I was diagnosed a few years ago with a rare autoimmune disease called Systemic Scleroderma. It caused a renal crisis and I was a dialysis patient for 5 years. I was also hospitalized for a year when the Scleroderma affected my stomach (stopped working) and injured my heart and lungs. I was sent home with Palliative Care to wait for Hospice. I had a feeding tube for a long time (in addition to other tubes, etc.) and I was bedbound. It is a miracle I am still alive… A little over a year ago, I was blessed with a kidney transplant. After a year of physical therapy, I walk again.

Before It's Too Late
Angel Garmon

Baby, I'm sorry,
That's what he says.
Looking so pitiful,
But grinning within.
You know that I love you,
But that is just an excuse.
To keep you there longer,
And prolong the abuse.
"I can't help it, I Love him"
That's what your heart says,
But who will raise your children?
Once you are dead!
You want to believe him,
"He has changed this time"
But who will guide you?
When he beats you blind!
There is no happy ending,
With a man full of hate.
You have to get out now,
Before it's too late!
You just want to be loved,
That's what you feel in your heart.
But you must first love yourself,
That is where it must start.
I know it's not easy,
I've been there before.
It took more than a beating,
For me to walk out that door.
I stayed and I stayed,
Waiting for change.
Until I looked in the mirror,
And didn't know my own name.

Who is that person?
I asked myself.
Once so full of life,
But now without.
I didn't know me anymore,
That's when it was time.
To walk out that door,
And never look behind.
Now I'm on my feet,
And I'm doing just great—
I got out then,
before it was too late.

Consent

SK Lockhart

the longing to write remains even as i fear what might be written. thoughts building into huge piles of feelings, tangled, fresh, raw.

something has broken inside me. it broke when i walked out of school a few months ago and it has spilled over now because of a case in the news of a rapist who will only spend a few months in a county jail. he raped an unconscious woman, stuck things in her vagina, was caught in the act. but he was a white, affluent athlete, he has promise—so he should not suffer.

the rage boils over, and i am tired of toeing the line. tired of holding it in. what the fuck?! all of the little incidents over the years burn in my skin. in my case, there was no jail time at all, no consequences whatsoever, except for the black man who broke in. he did deserve to be punished, but so did those fucking teenagers who first shamed me and used me as a sexual object. they were never punished. the white teens were never punished. my cousin was never punished. the men who grabbed my ass and grabbed my breasts, who stuck their fingers into my pants without permission, the men who leered. the ones who grabbed. the comments. the shame. the fear. *how come we assume that white men don't "mean" it?!* of course they do. they hold the power. they have no consequences….how can i simultaneously be so powerful that men "lose" control around my sexuality and yet so powerless that my consent is a non-issue?

too many to count. the endless comments, appraisals, and judgements about the sexual worth or beauty of each fucking body part. invisible rage. fear. will he rape me? i thought i said no. i thought it was clear. what did i do wrong? how the fuck is this my fault?

but i was drinking, we were drinking. i let him into my house. it's my fault, i was warned about him. it was harmless. i should be flattered. take it like a man. wtf?!! i am too sensitive. they can't help it. i asked for it. i want to fucking scream it all out. lay back and enjoy it.

don't be so uptight. don't be a prude. don't be frigid. don't be a tease. you were acting slutty.

taught to hide, to expose, to be the one who has to control it all. it makes me sick. i want to vomit every single moment out of my body. i am in control. i let it happen. i should have. i should not have. i must. rage, rage fucking rage. entitlement.

Out to Sea
Sherry L Jonckheere

Out to sea
Without a push
No rope untied
Or passage paid
Acres of uncertainty
Edges dark and unending

Yet here I am
Adrift in the unknown

Nothing in sight to remember where I began
Or to let me know where to go

The currents shift violently
Insides turn outward

Prying my grip from all solidity
An ocean of darkness waiting on surrender.

Collage of Scars
Alice Maldonado Gallardo

I have a collection
of subterraneous canals,
scars spreading apart,
pulsars radiating
the death of a great star.

Scars praying
in a congregation
of unspoken words.
Repressed sighs
of a broken life
left behind
on recycled
hospital beds,
and sacrificial
ambulance slabs.

Laments chiseled
and engraved
with my blood
on the sculpture
of a veiled skin.

Scars forming
a cauterized map
of a previous life,
untouched by wounds,
protected only by
the innocence of youth.

Only the best translator
can read
my book of scars
by finding the
lost reflection
of the solitary moon
deep in the dark
expanse of my eyes.

Silence Perpetuates Abuse
Carolyn Riker

I hear cries in the darkest of nights. I hear it at twilight and it's not in an alleyway but of ordinary pink and blue rooms. Abuse happens in the plain shades of real.

When the gut of quiet can release the pain stuffed deep, those words are a revolt. There's power boiling in words of truth. It creates scolding unease and many will try to deny and silence and admonish: "Don't bring the ugly to the surface. We'd rather wallow in the prettiness of pretending-everything-is-sickly-fine. Forgive and forget. Pray. Repent. Close your little mind. Nothing happened."

Silence perpetuates abuse. The insidiousness of it is deadly.

It's a felony of soul when no one believes in the abyss of someone's truths.

Shame and anguish become an arsenal of self-loathing and self-doubt manifests in a twisted day-nightmare: "Did the abuse really happen? Am I to blame? Did I walk or sit or eat the wrong way?"

A straightforward answer, "No, you didn't. You did nothing wrong. I believe in you and your story."

Shining light on the underbelly of deceit makes the shadows writhe; keep those words of truth coming. Let holy hell be exposed. I'm with you.

Teach and share early what is right.

Let children be safe and not afraid when the click of the light goes dark.

Let women walk with the swish of their skirts and let the mighty words of,

"No! Leave me the hell alone!" finally be heard.

(My Abusers) Did You Know?
Mariann Martland

With your hands around my throat, did you know
I would feel them in two decades time? That sometimes
living would feel like slow death
through the memory of hands in places that make me
shudder and shame in remembrance?

Your face stares at me, in the dark, just as you
imprinted. Tiny wrists, held, pushed down by the
weight of lies and bodies. When you fell limp on my tightly knotted corpse,
were you thinking of the fairies and butterflies
my eyes fixed upon on my wallpaper of dreams?

Can you remember the toxic smell of drink and dirt and
despair that filled your room as I ran away
in my mind, body frozen to the spot, rotting in your stench?
Dragged, pushed, trapped; bruises explained through accidental clumsy play.

Forced to pray to your god over a coffin filled with you, bowing
on the terrified knee of my body—dead and shriveled
before it had chance to grow. Pain, blood, violation, rape;
all sink into the background against the torment of a life taken.

I was special. Is that not what you told me?

The Bloodletting Ritual

Nancy Shiner

Razor's edge glints, preparing for the sacrifice.

Arms bared, shiver of skin fearing the cut, trembling in anticipation of pain's release. Heart pounds…fear, excitement, purge of emotion overload trembling on the edge of insanity's grip. I perform the ritual.

The altar must be prepared just so. Bathtub my temple, razor my priest, accoutrements laid out exactly so, sacraments to a body awaiting its baptism by fire. I step into the tub, hot soapy water kissing my waiting breasts, surrounding the cleft of the body that houses the pain of said parts' violation. I pray to the God of release to take me down tonight, neither death nor annihilation but simply the shedding of blood to anoint my skin with the purge of its agony unable to be contained.

My breath is now shallow; fear overwhelms, this cutting into skin and nerve not for the weak, though many consider it a sign of weakness. I have always been weak. I have never been weak. I know nothing other than the road to survival through any means necessary, even this bathing in blood which brings momentary relief.

My fingers shake. An act once performed with no physical sense now burns hot with electric sizzle as razor splits skin and opens to white meaty flesh below. Split skin does not immediately surrender its treasure. Blood wells up slowly, painfully; birthing itself through the layers in much the same way my soul births its pain to the release of blood-stained water surrounding.

Sharp scent of rust, so visceral I can taste its metallic bite on my tongue as it fills my nostrils. Inner chaos, the screaming emotions scrambling my head begin to slide into the darkened abyss of ritual's release as I float body-naked in a river of red. Praying to the god of pain to take me down tonight and bed me with its intimate caress upon body scarred. I have given its sacrifice, with body marked, blood's flow, nerves screaming in silent release.

The ritual concludes at sermon's end.

Body lays in blood-filled tub until the water chills and goosebumps war with opened skin. Cloth pressed to wound, I wrap it with bandage prepared, razor wiped down in preparation for next deity's call. Evidence erased as tub and floor become sacraments unstained, wiped down and ritual erased, gone in the recesses of a mind that knows too well how to make reality disappear—*truth becomes untruth before my blinded eyes.*

Legs now shake from effort and adrenaline's abandon. Pyjamas wrap desecrated limbs, covering proof of my connection to a past of ritual comfort, long sleeves my armour to protect against eyes too ready to condemn, too uncaring to rescue. I stumble to my room, lay body weary on sheets of white, untouched by sin. Ragged breath. Shame descends.

Finding Safety
Margo Stebbing

I was fourteen
and still made daisy chains
sitting on the grass with my friends.
I don't know how old he was,
I think still a teen wolf.
There, behind a schoolyard
overlooking my favorite canyon
where the horses were
stalled,
in my solitary time of refuge
walking home after school
the canyon of
my impressionist painting.

I used to call that my first sexual experience
until my friend told me:
that was not your first!
That was sexual abuse honey.

I wonder how many of us women
live with our stories
stuffed deep into the
back of our closets.

How many of us,
while walking alone on a path,
are looking from left to right
the sense of hypervigilance alone
in beautiful nature
just because,
you never know,
it might happen again.

Into the woods at grandmother's house
who can prepare a girl
for the predator
the wolf, the bluebeard,
the charming or not.
Offering to show you 'something'.
I still feel the frozen part inside of me,
hard to respond to other women's stories,
that place in me a hardened soldier
locked down
even now
after
all.
I
now
understand
why I wrote a poem about
93 million miles away yesterday
as that is where I automatically go
when triggered, into the infinite cosmos
to find safety.

Crimson
SK Lockhart

the little drops of deep red blood
soothe me
calm me
the cuts feel icy cold
a sharp contrast to the warmth that
seeps out
i know it's my blood
but at the time
it just seems curious
beautiful circles
against my light skin
that roll away
the throbbing that
i feel later on
reminds me that
my heart is still inside
beating
keeping me here
even when i feel
locked away
in another world
holding me prisoner
even when i want
to fade away into
nothingness

Author's note: First published in *Wild Beauty: Breathing Through the Storm* by SK Lockhart, Oct. 2016

The Anxiety That Holds
Mariann Martland

i'm wondering
where this life starts and where it ends. is it somewhere between
the inhale of a sharp breath and the wilting of a leaf, or drowning
in exhales while the sun gives rise to a new day?

it sometimes feels
like the world will come to a crashing end
if i don't solve a never ending equation
presenting itself to me on each raw nerve.
and it changes by the hour, new sums and divisions,
twisting and turning through the hallowed halls of my heart.
and i'm not done yet.
i am not done with this life,

this life that feels heavier than the moon, as it crushes my lungs
with each misplaced breath and lingering beat. and
she's shining; my moon, who lights my path home through
each long night i spend crying out my answers in the dark. but

the questions are louder, they call and
they cry and they scream through a voice that is mine.
i'm wondering when the noise stops, how this life starts anew
or when the last curtain falls.

The Empath Anthem
Dolly Mahtani

For years, the ignorance of being an Empath felt like a curse. I prayed for someone else to notice too. If there was a fire, at least it's something you could see and smell, you'd react immediately.

Call whoever you call in emergencies.

I pray for a world, for a future where a broken heart is treated just as gently as a broken arm. Where we don't need bravery to stand up and say to someone else "I'm not okay". A future where our health plan includes mental sick days. None of us are really, truly okay. We're all just trying our best. Falling down and getting back up again.

Let's be more compassionate. More honest. More open. How sad it is that we can hide it so well, that there are masks big enough and strong enough to hold all the shame, the guilt, the doubt, the fear within. Why? Why? Why? Why? Why?! I probably asked myself this question about a hundred times. *Why are we so far from where we want to be, why do we pretend to be okay, what the hell does that mean anyway?!*

I look at the old man sleeping on the streets and I know the drug addiction doesn't let him think of much else, but I once knew him and he wasn't always like this. He would be happy even if he had no home, no food or clothes, he'd be happy if he could get his daughter to look at him again.

That's the weight…

But you see that secretary at the bank? You could never tell but she loves to smile and let her hair down and go wild. Oh, you gotta see her dance. See that school teacher? He secretly thinks all his students are superheroes. That single mother? You don't need to worry about her. Lorelai Gilmore is her role model. That teenager that hides her face under her dark black hair? She's the smartest girl in the room. She's going to grow up to do great things, just give it time. That's the privilege.

I wouldn't have it any other way. That's just the way it is. We've been experiencing dichotomy ever since we entered these bodies. I've made my peace with the duality. If you want to feel, you gotta let it all in. I'll admit it does get to be too much. I feel defeated at times. I'm waving the white flag but nothing—the war goes on.

What do I do? I retreat. I go inward. I go silent. I go numb. I go deaf. I go dumb. Other times I break open, spill my heart out on the asphalt, I watch as little flowers grow along the sidewalk where the cracks once used to be. Other times I am the embodiment of mercy. I give what I have.

I give what I don't have. I give until it bleeds. I give it all away.

Most of all, I just sit and close my eyes and envision the light. I smile as I begin to feel the vibe of the beauty and love within me. The softness with which I think, act and speak. The power I have to fill myself with what I need. I am the best of me, I am the answer I seek. So are you. Can you see it? That light in you. Does it ache for love, peace and truth too? Wake up and ignite with me. Will you burn with me, my friend? Let us start a fire so bright it will burn all that is false to the ground. The land of truth will reign and here we are all sovereign.

Say What You Need To Say

Annie Dear

Tightly wrapped
around the scream
I smile and sit
quietly
toes tapping
stomach falling
anxiety mounting
the silence
presses in
and mutes me
And then your words
cut through the pain
'say it anyway'
you tell me
'say it anyway'
and I do
And the scream
hisses and fades
as the pressure
is released
And I add the sound
of my words
to yours
And together
we break the power
of the silence.

CHAPTER 7

WE ARE HER PROTECTORS

"The eyes of the future are looking back at us and they are praying for us to see beyond our own time. They are kneeling with hands clasped that we might act with restraint that we might leave room for the life that is destined to come. To protect what is wild is to protect what is gentle. Perhaps the wilderness we fear is the pause between our own heartbeats, the silent space that says we live only by grace. Wilderness lives by this same grace. Wild mercy is in our hands."

—Terry Tempest Williams, Refuge: An Unnatural History of Family and Place

At The Edge of a Season
Anita Acuna

Autumn crisps under my feet.
Silent air cracks my lungs.
No longer afraid of Autumn's dying.
Winter is dream time.
Earth is one big sleep
and we hurriedly float across her skin—
not hearing her heartbeat,
nor her faint breath,
or feel her stirring in her slumber.

Farthest Reach
BethAnne Kapansky Wright

Pollution
in the farthest reach
of the sea;
down deep in a world
still oft' unexplored,
and yet we have left
great footprints on
what once sat pristine.

How far will we go
before we realize
too much?
How long will we reach
before we see we've
overstretched?

How much will we
consume before we see
we can't sustain
this way of life where
we take and keep taking.

Our actions create
consequence
outside of just us,
each thought, act and deed
subtly shaping and weaving
life's web.

We can't undo
the reach we've leaved,

but we can work to change
our future weaves.
Bring back those streams
that once flowed clean.

If we want to be great
stewards, caretakers,
protectors of our nation
then we need to uphold life
more than we do
consumption and ambition—

So what once sat pristine
becomes cherished again
and not just a fading memory
in our imagination.

Poet's note: Previously published in *Heliotrope Nights*.

Beneath the Surface
Jody Kristine Johnson

I can't bloom freely in this arid landscape,
but my roots are deep and wide,
burrowing into the fertile ground
far beneath the surface
to gain strength and nourishment.
From above I am unimpressive,
small green stems and leaves
often eaten by predators
but from below I am massive;
a complex network of roots
that spans half a field,
a web of interconnected fibers
that touches all the life around me
in this hidden place.

Extinction
BethAnne Kapansky Wright

The skies
and the seas
and the grounds
and the bees
and the moon
and the trees
and the fish
and all those who be—

Can't we see we're not
more than or less than
but equal in?

And we are running
life out of this place
in our efforts to
expand,
when what we really
need to do is
contract—
listen, pay attention
to the breaks and
fissures in the heart
of this space.

Each stone we cast
into the pond creating
ripple effects
for those to come,
for we're all in danger
of extinction.

And if we don't
look up, link up, love up:
see the same
life graced pattern
running through
our veins…
we will miss this
precious chance to save
so much more than
just ourselves—

Redeem earth's face,
before she breaks.

Poet's note: Previously published in *Heliotrope Nights*.

If We Could Turn Back Time /Doomsday

Kai Coggin

(After Cher)

Good evening
from planet earth,
local time on the Doomsday Clock
is two and a half minutes to midnight,
midnight
is the end of humanity as we know it,
total obliteration of our little blue dot of hope,
the decimation of the human race,
by human hands,
by human bombs,
by human eyes
turning blinders to the faces of darkness,
midnight.

> We didn't really mean to do this,
> we really wanna see him go,
> he'll keep making us cry,
> and baby,
> If we could turn back time—
> If we could find a way
> We'd take back all the votes that elected him
> and he'd go away....

It's two and a half minutes to midnight.
A team of Nobel Laureates
at the Bulletin of Atomic Scientists
has used the Doomsday Clock

to track humanity's progress or lack of humanity
since 1945,
when war was still fresh on our lips,
when the rise of one mustached dictator
saw the slaughter of millions,
midnight,
tick tock, tick tock, midnight,
always this looming end on the horizon,
this mushroom cloud of vaporization by fire.

        If we could turn back time—
        If we could find a way.

In the last 72 years,
the minute hand has inched closer to midnight,

3 minutes to midnight in 1949
        when The Soviet Union tested its first atomic bomb,
2 minutes to midnight in 1953
        when the US tested its first thermonuclear device,
        an answer in fire,

through the cold war between the US and Russia,
nuclear
promises
pointed cold at each other's skies.

The minute hand has swung back and forth
through the ebbs of history,
the geopolitical factors that bond and break,
the hateful handful of men that hold human existence in their hands.

10 minutes to midnight in 1990
        when the Berlin Wall crumbled and the cold war ended,
17 minutes to midnight in 1991,
        Strategic Arms Reduction Treaty signed, Soviet Union dissolved.

This was our safest hour.

Fast forward through more swings
of humanity's minute hand fate
to 2017,
where our new white house resident embarrassment
calls for a nuclear arms race against Russia,
where a white nationalist extremist is his right hand man,
where a Muslim ban that's "not a Muslim ban"
has already infuriated nations against us,
where men acting like boys showing off
who's got the bigger toys
hold our collective future in their tiny hands.

> We didn't really mean to do this,
> we really wanna see him go,
> he's gonna make us all die,
> and baby,
> If we could turn back time—
> If we could find a way
> We'd take back all the votes that elected him
> and he'd go away…

Also swiped from the record of political truth
are the words and facts of scientific experts
regarding climate change,

CLIMATE CHANGE IS REAL.
say it with me now,
CLIMATE CHANGE IS REAL.

the world temperature is heating up,
the ice caps are melting,
the oceans are rising,
it's fucking 75 degrees in January,
we have contributed to our own destruction

but any alarming preventative eruptions
from the mouths of scientists are silenced!

The Environmental Protection Agency has a
red, white, and blue flag gag order in its mouth.
The National Parks are about to be raped and drilled for OIL!
Scientists, save your research
because
this orange little man is coming
for your files.
He will wipe out
our environment(all progress)
and fill the void with divisiveness and lies.

    "Words are like weapons they wound sometimes."
    We didn't really mean to do this,
    we really wanna see him go,
    he's gonna make us all die, and baby,
    If we could turn back time—
    If we could find a way.
    We'd take back all the votes that elected him
    and he'd go away.
    If we could reach the truth,
    I know just what we'd do,
    we'd move back all the minutes inching closer
    to save me and you…

Good evening
from planet earth,
local time on the Doomsday Clock
is two and a half minutes to midnight.

Autumn Haikus

Anita Acuna

Forest creek flowing
A lone leaf tumbles along
Waters sing of fall.

The pond lies serene
framed in golden hues while fish
dart among the leaves.

Dawn's gentle rising
Songs of birds herald the day
Toad rests on a stone.

A cold, damp morning
Sun shines through the sparkles of
The bare, webbed branches.

Moonlight twisting through branches.
I am silver washed.
Radiant. Clean. Pure.

Home
Kathryn Brown Ramsperger

We only came in summer then.
Plucking scuppernongs,
Peeling off their thin red skins,
We felt for seeds in their translucent wombs,
Popped their sour sweet into our mouths.

The woman said to me,
You'll be back.
This is your mother's home.
I could not see her.
The sun shone on my face.

They left me and returned to the vines.
They live in one frame house
And nurse another.
Settled in country air, country ways.
But I fly in, then out again.

I found the trap my brother set.
A wooden box, its hinges
Rattled in cold, knee-high wheat.
I unleashed the creature inside,
Gray fur splattered with rusty blood.

Today, I discovered the hole she'd gnawed,
And only then
Remembered
The frightened blank of her eyes.

Fleeting

Judi Lenehan

Wrapped in your warmth
Memories surround me
Hands held, hands covered in dirt.
Daffodils open and bright
Annual, fragile, seen, unseen.

Bird song, soft tender grass, a perfectly beautiful sea and sky colored robin's egg placed innocently, naively back into the nest.

Home is ephemeral.

The sound of rain, the heaviness of sleep. A ginger cat clown I could not keep.

Pan fried pork chops, dripping sweet red tomatoes, crisp buttery corn, and a vase holding a solitary wildflower.

Swirling steam, lemon lift tea, waiting for fears, for dreams, for life to unfold.

Youth is ephemeral

Towels folded three by three, tucked neatly, worn and smooth a children's book, the story rhythmic and comforting.

Fleeting.

Deconstructing Darwin
Cari Greywolf

Murky darkness swirls across the primeval forest floor.
Wet moss clings to dying trees, wresting life out of death.
Fruit from the forbidden tree of knowledge buries our
truest knowing, deep, out of sight, no headstone or marker.

Complacency settles in now.
Apples a dime a dozen,
cheap as ignorance
sucking intuition from our bones.

Far above the forest's canopy,
beyond human visual capacity,
from a free fall, rip cord pulled,
a parachute opens
a refugee holding tight to
what little wisdom remains
a deep breath exhaling ancient memories
of truth and rightness. Gravity pulls
down hard. Drop and roll, she remembers vaguely,
and drop and roll she does across the dry
forsaken earth, seeking sustenance and justice
an exile holding a last fleeting glance of a life
unarmored, enamored in false security and safety.

Face to face with the barren ground, an
ephemeral recollection of lush grasses
emerges from her panicked mind, a tease
of what was and may never be again.

She feels herself shrivel hot day after
freezing night, no longer able to stand.
Crawling lizard-like, seeking out hiding places,
witnessing her de-evolution from mammal
to reptile, conscious awareness evaporating
with each breath until there is no self,
only pure instinct—survive 'til the next inhale.

Inshallah
Margo Stebbing

Enduring
the absence of light
on a night sea voyage,
Delft blue skies follow
torrential rains.

Inshallah

White clay cliffs mirrored in
the many eyes of deep umber,
people whose crumbling
homelands disappear into
indigo prayers for safety.

Inshallah

Toward a sea hungry
for prayers and sacrifice,
flee the midnight blue people
crowded in their boats,
seeking
the colors of mercy.

Inshallah.

And so on we go,
in this great shifting time,
we live
by fire in the flames
of the Kali Yuga;

Who are we— the people of the Promised Land
in the great neutral colorless tide?
A people avid for yoga, non-gmo food
endless milk and honey
yet mired in non-engagement
while the poison seeps deep
and we all know it.

What then,
is the color of mercy for us?
What hues will penetrate
the cultural anesthesia and disconnect
between what we love
and what we must save?

God is willing,
but are we?

Inshallah.

Editor's note: Inshallah means "God is willing"

Duwamish
Judi Lenehan

Green river
edges
eddies and currents
mammoth machines peer down
ships like sharks
prowling
a road curling and straddling
a current of commerce
rippling, ripples and riffles
a nation once fed
now divided
dispersed
channeled to unfamiliar places
promises made, promises broken
offered a life, given a token
people of the inside
spread-out.

Song of Oshun

Anita Acuna

Daily I go outdoors to greet the day, I call it my ritual commune with Nature. I am blessed to live at the edge of a forest with a creek that runs along the property. As I sit by the creek I am flanked by three large maples which I've adopted as my *guardian trees*.

I spend time expressing gratitude for my life, my surroundings, and all that has yet to come in my life. Mornings and twilight are my favorite times at creekside. I've memorized every dip and gurgle as the water tumbles over the rocks.

This one night was quiet—but for the creek. As I took in the serenity, watching the twilight sky morph in its hues, I heard another sound. It was faint, but distinct. A humming tone. I strained, finally pulling off my hoodie to better hear. Yes, there it was again, HUMMING! The tones lilted and fell and had the quality of a woman's voice. It was most definitely a song being hummed, so very faint yet distant amidst the sounds of creek waters.

Mesmerized I continued to listen, not moving a muscle. For a few solid minutes this song drifted. It was unmistakably coming from the creek! I believe that I was blessed to hear the song of an Elemental or the freshwater Goddess herself, Oshun. A rare treat indeed.

Individuals such as the founders of the Findhorn Community, Marko Pogacnik, Nathaniel Altman and others who've had regular contact with various Elementals, share a message. The Elementals will make themselves known once again as humankind pours their energies into restoring Mother Earth. Every rock, tree, plant, and water source require our efforts to nourish, safeguard, and ultimately provide balance.

As we move in nature with respect and integrity, we feed the sentient life forms all around us with our energies, our love. We can offer small tokens of honor such as requesting permission before cutting a plant and expressing gratitude when the plant heals us or provides nourishment.

When you stand before the ocean and sense its power in the surf, when you watch the trees dance and groan against the windstorm, when the scent of a flower intoxicates you, when the majesty of a mountain range leaves you in awe, then you have connected with the all-encompassing energies of every sentient being, its devas, and elementals. *Welcome home.*

Editor's note: Oshun, is an *orisha*, a spirit or deity that reflects one of the manifestations of God in the Ifá and Yoruba religions. Oshun is a Nigerian Yoruba deity of the river and freshwater, luxury and pleasure, sexuality and fertility, and beauty and love. She is connected to destiny and divination. (Source: Wikipedia)

Habitat
BethAnne Kapansky Wright

We only have one earth. One planet. One space.
One land of blue and green and life that we all
must inhabit and grace.

What will we do when she's gone?
Can you see, will you see, please see, please believe—

We can't sustain this way of life where we take
without giving.

We can't sustain this way of life where we take
without giving.

We can't sustain this way of life where we take
without giving.

I wrote that letter to the senators today,
and yesterday,
and the day before,
and I'm losing track
of all the letters I'm writing,
the money I'm sending,
the petitions I'm signing.

*How is it what's evil can be disguised as good
and so many people seem to be buying?*

Have we become so disconnected from the source
that we cannot hear the places where humanity
is dying?

Have we lost so much of who we are we can't hear
the sounds of our own souls crying?

I go each day and sit with my trees,
press my face to the earth
(it hurts, it hurts, everywhere it hurts),

She tells me all life holds value from the greatest to the least.
That hope can be found in the origins of a seed.
To never give up on being the change we need.

And mostly she reminds me to keep the one space clean,
which I will need to inhabit so I can love, care and believe—

I heed her words, sit with her, and we listen to the beat
of each other's hearts.

All circles are sacred within the hoop of life. ♥

CHAPTER 8

I BELIEVE

"The longing to tell one's story and the process of telling is symbolically a gesture of longing to recover the past in such a way that one experiences both a sense of reunion and a sense of release."

—BELL HOOKS

Circle of Women
Robin Baldwin

In this circle of women
I am rich in spirit
I am fortified in soul
I am graced in peace.
In this circle of women
I am forgiven,
I am understood,
I am accepted.
In this circle of women
I am free,
I am vulnerable,
I am me.

She Who Will Fly
Tammy T. Stone

I can see myself there in the distance,
carved in absentia, the shape of a girl
small, wispy, soft around the edges,

Not sure of her footing; nor can she fly.
Instead she makes her first discovery,
the power of the look, eye on the world.

Fixed in the land of the unseen, she sees.
A gaze outward from a place between
the stars and sand and dying embers.

She sees, but she knows not what to do.
Her outreached hand meets no hand,
petals close softly in her young heart.

It aches. She reaches down to smother
herself in the fragrant, dense earth,
as if to beg her presence of the world.

She does not know why she does this,
or how she can get from there to here,
from the cosmic dust that made her,

To a creature pulsing with raw fever
dancing for the fallen and the nascent,
bowing with thanks for her emergence.

Yes! It is to see: the garden of my life!
It's messy and threatens to dissolve her,
but she loves it madly and it never does.

The Reluctant Shaman
BethAnne Kapansky Wright

Nobody who is called to this path
wants to walk it.

It is not for the faint of heart
or thin of skin
or the ones who seek ease or acceptance
or those who'd stall when soul gives call.

It comes at a cost
—a ripping of your seams—
(and maybe more than once, two times,
three times, *so many times I've lost count*)
so Life can keep taking you apart
and make the room to stretch your heart.

Teach you about what is real.
Teach you the mystery of change.
Sweep you up into a city of clouds
where you see the darkness, the burning, the hurting, the pain—
see the great need
for peace
for healing
for love
in the staunched flow of humanity's veins.

You'll be bade to go down deep,
find your pearls amongst dark sediment,
charged to face the shadow selves
and learn the grace of penitence,
"there but the grace of love go I"
these words become your catechist,

and you can't be anything but true—
fierce authenticity your regiment.

You will find yourself to lose yourself.
Learn to become to be undone.
And just when you've reached a stasis of place,
Life will ask you to leave that comfort zone,
pack up your heart to learn new space.

I wouldn't wish this path on anyone,
it is some of the loneliest steps I ever walked.

And yet I have many guides, unseen by the eyes,
the trees are my friends and my spirits the sky,
I see the love laced web connecting you—
and all that lays between— and I.
So reluctant steps with faithful bent
(you really can't ignore the insistent soul's intent)
I keep stepping towards the light.

Ancient Hymns of Her
Sonja Phillips

She is awakening to the songs of her inner goddess.
She is learning to dance in her own darkness.
She is chanting a new song, daring to be different.
Beneath the quieted moon, undisturbed.
Lost in the ancient hymns of her.
I hear a voice that is mine, and another.
A timeless rhythm, within the depths of my soul.
I came to know her.
We are one in nature.
Her, the other within.
She has taken me to a place of solace,
the deep inner knowing that lives within me,
I wish never to return, reclaiming the power once held by her.
Her divine light is emerging,
the goddess has returned.
From her lips to my heart.
Her best intentions are kindled by something
more than flesh can touch,
more than words can obtain,
She is lifting us into the highest forms of love.
She is wounded but loves so deeply.
Estranged from the gods, her love diminishes not.
She sings on, resurrecting the Eden within herself.
I hear the song of a goddess.
Aligning with the inner rhythms of nature.
Aligning with the soft anthems of the sky.
I can hear the musical intonations of the universe in her being.
Her enchanting music uniting the inner and outer realms.
Beneath the quieted moon, undisturbed,
a universal song of love.
Lost in the ancient hymns of her.
My inward journey is just a
wandering home.

The Wall That Divides Me from Myself

Ilda Dashi

This is dedicated to everyone *but especially to those women who are in their own journey* of discovering their beings and realize that the truth of the innermost core is much better than the superficial persona who is shown to the world. It is time to allow and embrace our inner beings!

There is a wall between me and myself. On one side of it, I see a naked body covered with dust laying down on the floor with her two feet raised up tight to her knees and her hands holding her two legs together.

She wants to be seen. She is craving to be exposed. She is longing to be let out in the open like air to breathe and live.

On the other side of the wall there is another female figure dressed in black and white, having a stick in her hands—like if she was a judge or a punisher of some kind. Her black high heels make noise as she directs the orchestra that oftentimes is being played out there in the public. This white and black lady wants to have the supremacy over the other naked, fragile one.

There's a lot more genuine and sincere in the naked female figure. She touches her breasts softly as she holds her legs with one of her hands. Her energy is primal, primitive and pure.

She drinks water and it falls all over her body, making her wet but she enjoys it; she likes to see her body wet. Her hair wet. Her cheeks and lips wet and red as the sun rises and sets every day.

She plays with her hair as she watches her eyes in the piece of glass that is near her left foot. She admires her nudity and she is not ashamed of her curves and nakedness. She enjoys and she makes love to it softly and widely with that image of herself. She knows no rules. She just is.

While the other lady in black and white tries to suppress her, to repress her for fear of not existing anymore. The black and white figure criticizes. She punishes the other naked female figure. She yells at her. Screams at her face which she sees at these small holes through the wall.

The light enters through these small holes from both sides yet it shines brightly where the naked female figure is standing because she knows that to be truly true one needs to get naked. Nude in front of one's eyes. Open up and allow the light to raise her up. She knows that she does not need clothes to cover herself. *She needs nothing for she herself is the truth of her existence and ready to be revealed and exposed under the sun's light.*

She is coming out. She is finding new ways to come out nude as she is; uncovered but beautiful and real. She is not scared of her nakedness. Nor of her small breasts. Nor of her fat thighs because she knows those are exactly as she needs them to be—beautiful in their own way!

She never criticizes. She just wants to enjoy life to the fullest. She is coming out! Breaking this fucking wall!

Trust Me on This
Robin Baldwin

My dear beautiful daughters,
There is so much I want to say.
You both amaze me every day.
By the time you read this you'll
Be 13, officially teenagers!

First, I want you to know that
This too shall pass.
Whatever negative feelings
Or experiences you have now
Will not last forever
Even though it feels that way.
Trust me on this.

Believe in yourself because
You are worth it.
You are worth knowing
You are worth loving
You are worth living.
Trust me on this.

It's okay to say no
To drugs, bullying, racism,
Smoking, drinking, and
Sex before you're ready for it.
Trust me on this.
Always stay true to yourselves
And let that be your guide.
I know you both figured this out
In third grade but it bears repeating
While you're in the throes of adolescence.
Trust me on this.

Treat others with respect
By living the Golden Rule
At all times.
Trust me on this.

Live life out loud
With open hearts and
Lots of laughter.
Life is too short to
Be serious or sad.
Trust me on this.

Find your own happiness
In whatever you do
And success will follow.
Trust me on this.

Don't be afraid to fail.
That's how we learn and grow.
And Dad and I will still love you!
Trust me on this.

Love will take you on many roads
But when you've found the one
To spend your life with
You will know.
Trust me on this.

Through it all, love yourself.
For this forms the foundation for
Self-confidence, courage,
Joy and passion.
Trust me on this.

All my love,
Mom

Unveiling the Mystery
Sonja Phillips

I am from somewhere... I am from nowhere... I am a stranger in a faraway land. On a journey beyond self, I am the love that cannot be unfelt... I am the one of many... traveling through many different places, and many lifetimes. I am your unbridled thoughts. I am the words that touch deeply within. Unveiling the mystery... *I am the ancient truths stirring in the winds.*

We are Women
Robin Baldwin

We are women
From different places
In time, country, and life,
With different loves, sorrows, joys.
We are wives, daughters, moms, grandmothers,
Friends, colleagues, mentors.
We have our own stories to tell
Of pain and triumph,
Loss and acceptance,
Depression and hope.
We have faced incredible tragedies
That have broken us,
Torn us apart,
Shattered our spirit.
We are survivors of a society
That wants to see us fail,
To be put in our places,
To lose ourselves for the sake of others.
From the depths of our souls
We knew we would not give up fighting for
Justice
Equality
Humanity
For what's right
For what's true
For what's fair.
We are sisters joining forces
Showing the world
That we will not back down.
We will be heard
We will prevail
We shall overcome
We are women.

Dogma
Molly Moblo Perusse

Once I was afraid.
I thought I didn't have a voice.
Well, I had a voice,
It rambled in a constant negative gibberish with
one desired outcome, "Somebody loves me."

Reliant on external commendation, approval of right or wrong doing.
Memories of people walking away while I was speaking.
An inner dialogue of self-doubt and loathing.
A religious foundation based on original sin, laying
the blame of separation on the female.
A dichotomic God who was omnipotent, omniscient, omnipresent,
And yet begged to be feared, absolution
only through priestly mediation.
An oxymoronic message.
A needy love/hate existence.
A warped world perception in a low grade vibration.
A chasm of disconnection, of misunderstanding,
between Adam and Eve.
A dogged divine feminine rearing its unbalanced head

In a life of *reality* shows playing on the shadow victim archetype.
A euphoric existence seemed beyond my reach
But, there was always a glimmer of bliss
shining through all questioning of
"Why am I here and what is my purpose?"

I became cognizant of an inner compass
*And birthed a new voice of the Goddess; one
without fear, of self-love and connection.*
I learned to tone the negative voice down,
shut it off, refine the flawed opinion,

The over-inflated worthlessness
Into a song of praise with lyrics of love.

I remembered my cheerleading skills while practicing
positive mantras in the mirror, and started
Yelling for the soul team of my birth.
That team included everyone, because all are God/
Goddess disguised in different costumes
Braving an excruciating, breathtaking, exhilarating human life
In order to experience duality, dichotomy, polarity.
I brave a promising voice full of belief in a true existence of oneness
And love without condition.
I strive to embody the transcendental Divinity.
Every day a blessing of choice, every thought a manifestation
Drawing synchronicity like a magnet, for better
or worse, until death us do part.

Amen.

An Attitude of Gratitude
Dolly Mahtani

I thank the mother that broke my heart.
The father that broke my pride.
The girl who never chose me but wouldn't let me leave.
I thank the grandfather who found me disgusting. I thank him
    so deeply.
I thank the aunt who thought I was not worthy of love.
I thank the teacher who gave up on me.
I thank the man who tried to rape me.
I thank the friend who committed suicide.
I thank the drunken nights and all the times I lost myself
    in someone else's mouth.
I thank the tequila and occasional salt.
I thank my best friend who used me for money.
I thank everyone always saying 'no' to me.
I thank the holy hole I crawled into to escape it all.
I thank the binge eating. The bulimia. The anorexia.
I thank the mental institute she sent me to.
I thank the depression and suicide attempts.
I thank poverty.
I thank not having anybody to help me.
I thank the unworthiness.
I thank the cheating. I thank the beating. I thank the abuse.
I thank the drugs. The LSD and E.
I thank the pride. I thank the ego. I thank the fear. I thank the shame.
    I thank the guilt.
I thank it all.
I am all of this. I am none of it.
I thank it all.
I am this moment. I am everything I want to be.
I am love. I am love. I am love.
I am free. I am free. I am free.
I am peace.

The Child Within Needs Gentle Care

Annie Dear

And I settle into
the stillness
and draw its quiet folds
around me
and the darkness
gathers
and I am not afraid
And the child
tucks in beside me
—abandoned still—
and we light
the flickering candles
and consider
the shadowy room
And the books whisper
and my words gather
and the blank screen
is silenced
and we are alone
And the tendrils stir
deep within her
and the fear tries
to waken
but there is nothing
to fear
in the still quiet room
And waiting quietly
I listen to the stillness
and the child within
and her gentle distress
and I wonder if her fear
will ever leave us
alone.

Crossroads
Robin Baldwin

The push-pull of my
Spiritual life wears on me
As my connection with God
Ebbs and flows.
I am trying to find
My self,
My purpose,
My faith,
My God.
Feeling adrift in a spiritual desert,
I yearn for something more
That I can't describe
But know I need to fill
This emptiness inside.
Standing at the crossroads
Of joy and sadness,
Faith and hope,
And everything in between
I pray to stop this churning
Of emotion and doubt
To find what I'm looking for.

Addiction
Kathryn Brown Ramsperger

You whip in and out of my life
Like a slender switch.
I see you as a pale smile,
A burning candle wick too close to wax,
A fading wave of light in a cavernous pool,
A seashell sound,
A persistent midnight thief.

You slide silent out of my sight
Like a star on a cloudy night,
And I squint and search once more.

If I find you,
I feel my hand might glide through you
And touch air
In this cage of illusion,
Each bar succumbing,
Another immediately beyond.

Some live for inheritance,
Waiting for wills and deeds
To reap forth fortunes.
Others have the gods of religion
Or the muses of self-knowledge.
Some strive for mountains
Some for words or songs or dance.

I have you.
We will all die in the end.

Battle Cry

Sherry L Jonckheere

Too feminine to be heard, too smart to be seen
This paradox a female ride through world's hellish scene.

Raging, speaking, standing strong
Another twist of mortals wrong.

Bending, remolding, and just trying to fit in
Yet all efforts bring hate, sexism and earthly sin.

Our hearts bloodied and bruised
With attempts volleyed yet fooled.

Our cries maligned, rejected and abused
As alt-masculinity continues on confused.

We have forgotten our soulful selves
True strength lies on dusty shelves.

Waiting to be taken
And out of sleep shaken.

Rise soul sisters and friends
To the call of wild hearts and mend.

We are enough
We are feminine tough.

No more powerful people have I met
Than women who refuse to give up yet.

We have done it all
With frayed dignity and stood tall.
Our power is born of overcoming defeat
Bursting forth still loving and complete.

We will not go back
As chattel and tack.

Our time is now
To take the long awaited bow.

No reason to delay
You can stomp and bay.

Our momentum is unstoppable
Our unity impenetrable.

No more jokes
Enough have pushed this false hoax.

We will not be silenced
Or abused or harnessed.

The past has shaped our unyielding will
And we have you to thank for your willingness to kill.

Being a woman is no easy thing
When the world gets lost in usury and bling.

We will not go back to quiet and pain
Forward we march to equality and sane.

Come forward all genders, all races and forms
Stand together now to challenge unjust norms.

Bring clear hearts and fierce voices
Filled with humanity's compassion and limitless choices.

Stand together with common cause
To transform primitive and demeaning laws.
I bring myself, embattled and scarred
To strengthen our bonds forever unmarred.

There is no tomorrow if we don't truth today
And say enough to what was and the archaic way.

There is only Now and it is time
To join as one and end the crime

Of degradation, ism's and hate
And blend our strength, hearts and voices
to embrace our equal state!

CHAPTER 9

JUSTICE SPEAKS

"There is work to do; that is why I cannot stop or sit still. As long as a child needs help, as long as people are not free, there will be work to do. As long as an elderly person is attacked or in need of support, there is work to do. As long as we have bigotry and crime, we have work to do."

—Rosa Parks

I'll Write a Song

Carolyn Riker

I'll write a song like no one has ever heard—*but they feel it*. It'll play in the heart of humankind. It'll be more than words but a living beauty, set to a tone of respect and equality. Tears and joy will be in solidarity. History will be honored and black and brown lives that never mattered will. The gifts, native to America will be succulent notes soaked in the seeds of sprouting soul.

I feel a song of justice and children will sing the harmony. I will honor the young and the aged will bestow the woodwind of wisdom from the marrow of their bones. Homeless will have a home. The infringed and ignored voices of obscurity will break the sound barrier of ordinary.

Schools won't be a pipeline to prison and the tenacious scar tissue of fettered pain will unfold shocking gifts of hell untold.

I will share my song. It is my dream and my dream is my hope. I will walk along the cobbled stones of distant and dusty lands and touch the essences of something I can't explain or see but can feel in the rhythm of my soul.

This song will never end. Let's join hands.

After the Election
Linda Webber

Darkness is here.
Again.
Embraced by the soft breast of the dark Mother,
I fold into the underworld.

Undone. Trumped.

Unknown.
Settling into Stillness.

Waiting.

Still (in two parts)
Kai Coggin

I.

I find myself lately
using the word
        still
like
there are still flowers,
there are still trees,
there is still laughter,
there is still the silent moon
        that watches our dark movements
there are still moments of wonder
        that can take your breath and turn it magic
        a lake freezing,
            the sounds it echoes from beneath the changing surface,
        how nature is a constant source of abundance
        despite how human our sorrow

  still
  still
  still

as though something has been robbed
as though something is missing
that we can't get back
desperately clutching for
    what   we let slip away,
a piece of humanity

a
peace
    a
    peace

        peace.

II.

Stillness—

this is not the time to stand still,
this is not the time to be still,
to meditate,
to wait
to wish
to withdraw
this is the moment that we define ourselves
    from the sketches we made on cave walls,
how have we grown?
    eons under our feet
    and still we cannot separate ourselves from
    what breaks us apart?
what does evolution taste like
if not the shape of speaking out on our tongues
    against the unholy wills of greedy men,
the mouth of protest against a demagogue,
the resistance and pushing back at every turn,

this is no time for stillness

this is no time for stillness

for what is still stays the same
and we cannot afford
this dark turn away from the sun
we cannot be still
in the face of a trigger happy nuclear thumb
we cannot be still
when the rights of women are reverted into submission
we cannot be still
when the billionaires grow fat off the sweat of the starving poor
we cannot be still
when freedoms of the press are compromised and truth is a second
class citizen
we cannot be still

when every movement he makes is a direct threat
to the decency that makes up our fibers as evolved human beings

they casted their votes on cave walls

but we stand in the face of the sun, we stand in our own light.

Without real leadership, the people will lead.

Days of Dickens and Hobbes
Cari Greywolf

Awakening from fanciful dreams
of elves and lush verdant forests.
Lingering in fertile sensations
of bygone youth and hopefulness.
Savoring the remaining moments
of peace 'ere reality breaks through.

My country 'tis of thee,
you I do mourn.

On the brink of doom
impending, impacting,
a colossal meteor
hurtling from the inside.
Unstoppable disaster.

Try as hard as we might,
darkness is descending.
The days of Dickens and Hobbes return
where the poor are banished
and there is no greater good.

The greed of power
and the gods of money
rule from the high peaks
of false magnitude
while the reigning wizard
drools naked in pools of fool's gold
babbling incongruities,
spewing hatred,
sewing fear.

We gather and plan our resistance,
trusting the slender threads of light
flickering inside to guide us through.

Many wonder "will it be enough?
Can we survive the madness
and vindictive pettiness of tyranny?"

Voices of Truth

Carolyn Riker

Let's stand strong. Hands touching the hearts against racism. We will NOT, and cannot be silenced. Voices of truth, over the malice of evil segregation. Let's talk to each other. Keep the dialogues open. Even on days when we feel discouraged, it is paramount to clip the snarled tangle of fears. It's a lie and a soul-binding cry.

Let's tell it, "STOP!" Listen! And feel!

We know truth is at the tip of the edges of heart. Let's see beyond the ranks of toxic political BS. Let's take steps together onto the platform of 'We [ARE] the People.' I am. You are. WE are ONE. We bleed shades of crimson life's blood.

I will not follow the crowd of a homogenized ordinary. I believe in a deep, soul-fulfilling democracy for all. Let's touch into the palette and shades of skin. Let's bow in respect and raise our arms in a loud, Shalom! Allah! Amen! The gods and goddess are of many. We are each intelligent and divine.

Let's turn the faucet on to our talents and let the uniqueness fill our starved souls with the sound of unity. The borders erased by the song of peace. Let the political preponderance of said, patriarchal hit an Alt-Ctrl-Del and cease such hatred, blame and violence.

Let's stand side by side, arms interlocked into a paradox of rebellious freedom with, respect and above all—LOVE.

Day 1: In Response to T.S. Eliot
Margo Stebbing

I am homeless in the narrow alleys of this Dark City
in this time of man,
my forehead furrowed, my eyes wet
in response to my ever shifting tribe, and
kin who are far, far away.
My ancestors hover behind me with words
I am not equipped to hear, though the hidden great birds
are roosting in trees high above my line of sight
yet I cannot hear them,
and in despair I find
my canoe is splintered.

I squat over a makeshift fire burning
in a five gallon drum of verse,
the busy street corner awash in unnatural noise as
people walk by and avert their gaze
to this unwelcome assault on the world,
for it is finally unmasked.
The heft and weight, like unfamiliar ballast
leans on our souls in its truth-telling,
and all the many platitudes we have gathered
fall like tin pennies in a beggar's empty can;
those words that have not lifted their weight of sorrow
and the hollow images of beauty meant to stir,
are of bulimic youth who are as lost to the state of grace
as unfledged birds, wings without muscle
and they fail soundlessly
to the task of flight.

Do I dare disturb the revered circles to say that
the ways to the promised land are hawked and sold
by the charismatic hucksters, for a fee,

and the idealization they promote
divorced from an imperfect humanity,
cleaves the natural being so that it is no longer
recognizable to itself, but forged of many masks
meta layers deep.

We live in the sky of our awareness
and by the pull of the dark loam of our animal natures
distracted by the lesser union of the
feminine and masculine, high and low,
and all the while, the great marriage to be forged
always
was between the dark and the light.

To find and to heed the call of the sacred camps,
the Standing Rocks of earth's defense,
as it has presented itself within our Anima Mundi,
the World Soul, the Great Basket—
the intrinsic connection between all living things.

As we row through the muddy waters with our twinned oars
learning to row together
alternating strokes of creation and disintegration,
to find the center that holds.

For every feeling will be visited upon you now
the ashes will be smeared upon your brow
for we have entered the night of our lifetime
though not without hope, the weight of
the unfathomable translation
is upon every single one of us
demanding the great rendering of meaning
and response;

We must not ignore the darkness
but ask of it
what is it that must be seen by the light
of the great bonfires that are burning within

and without,
for we must dare to disturb the universe
and in the discomfort, awake.

Yet, like Prometheus who stole fire from the gods once before,
let us bring the flames of fire to earth once again,
but this time,
teach ourselves and our descendants
how to use fire
without burning down the world.

Poet's note: I wrote this after Trump was elected, and was trying to give words to the weight I felt. The line from T.S. Eliot's poem I respond to is from: *The Love Song of J. Alfred Prufrock*: 'do I dare disturb the universe'.

We Will Come To Love

Maureen Kwiat Meshenberg

Though hatred would like
to steal our moment from us
peace will deliver her voice
of freedom
yes carried on
the winds of deliverance
we will come to love

though fear tries to choke
the tears of our grieving
let them fall like
holy water upon
the path of our creating
making our way
to come to love

though darkness tries to blind us
the eyes of our souls
see clear through the light
pass the dim
pass the treacherous
pass what appears to
be our destruction
we will rise to love

though some may try
to divide us
conquering our heart's battle cry
our battle will come
with the sword of truth
the shield of light

the breastplate of justice
we will clasp hands in unity
and we shall come to love

Poet's note: This is a poem I wrote the day after the Election in November 2016.

Those Geese Are Mean
Sherry L Jonckheere

And she said, "Those geese are mean!"
She is a kind soul.
A person who finds the good in all.
Someone for whom life is cushioned without fail.
Yet in a world filled with wars,
Greedy, soulless men,
And the planet on which we live
Exhausted by abuse and neglect,
She is unsettled by a bird.
Next to a beautiful early morning lake,
On a spectacular fall-colored day,
She is adamant to say out loud,
"Those geese are mean."

Breaking the Silence

Beverly Collier

All Black Americans bear the brunt of racism! Among the truths that many well-meaning whites don't seem to understand is that absolutely no Black American, regardless of his or her status or wealth, is spared from being the victim of racism on any given day. They live in a country where their character is judged by the color of their skin. Racial profiling, police harassment, false arrest, and brutality are a reality for them! *Perhaps the worst injustice is living in fear that they or their children will not return home as they are potential targets for violence, imprisonment, or even death every time they leave the house!*

It is important to understand the difference between racism and prejudice. We all have prejudices, regardless of the color of our skin. White people, however, own most of the wealth in this country and control almost all of our economic and social institutions. *Racism equals prejudice plus power.* White people not only have the power in this country; they benefit from the institution of systematic racism and therefore enjoy white privilege.

If white people could walk in the shoes of a person of color they would see the racism that they deal with every day. How can we continue to pretend it does not exist? Think about what it might be like to be the target of injustice and inequitable treatment just because your skin is black. How does it feel to be that one black person in the break room at work surrounded by white folk who don't have a clue about what your life is like? What it is like to compete in a predominantly white world where your best is never enough—where there is a different set of rules and expectations that you must follow in order to be successful and enjoy a quality life?

> *The roots of racism run deep. It is so ingrained in the white psyche that most of us whites live with the illusion of superiority. It is wrong! It is immoral! It is hurtful! It is deadly! We must resist racism! We must speak out*

against it! We must relinquish our white privilege when an inequitable situation arises.

It is the responsibility of white people to collectively stand up against racism. It starts within our own families, circle of friends, and communities. We must call out racism at every opportunity as we witness it in our daily lives. We must be vigilant when people of color are racially profiled or otherwise treated unjustly. We must demand justice and equality from our government officials and exercise our power to ensure that human rights are honored and valued.

Most white folks don't want to see nor hear about the dark side of our history, but we need to be reminded of just how brutal and cruel we have been in our oppression of black people. We need to recognize that it may look different now, but oppression of our black brothers and sisters is still occurring in this system of institutional racism that we have created and continue to participate in. We must never tell black people to just get over it!

Awakening to and acknowledging the evils of racism are only the first steps. Moving into action to make real change is crucial. *We must each do our part to eradicate this evil by learning to use our white privilege to dismantle the system of institutionalized racism block by block.* This system continues to thrive in our society today to the detriment of people of color. Each of us needs to take action based on our individual talents, monetary means, influence, and circumstances! We all have a responsibility to take action! We must step out of our comfort zones, deal with our white fragility and listen to our Black brothers and sisters as they share their life experiences and stories. We must stand with them in this struggle. It is the right and moral thing to do!

For me personally, I have found that once I had the courage to speak out against racism, I was no longer able to remain silent! The flames of passion for truth and justice drives my voice and actions! I find myself empowered and surrounded by others who seek truth and justice as well. I no longer fear what others think because I know that I am on the side of what is just and what is morally right!

I believe that we must all work to break this silence and stand united against racism! It is the only way to provide equality and justice for all our citizens!

Where Democracy Rises
Carolyn Riker

It starts with a sensation,
usually beneath the breastplate
that space unseen but felt
the tear spot of infinity
the raw and real of humanity
where noise is quiet
and solitude echoes a voice;
trees always hear
and the sea breathes through
the stretches and curves
of intuitiveness
until
vocal chords
contract and breach
the consciousness
simultaneously tears tremble with sea
this
to me
is where democracy rises
soul to soul
and we see.

Poet's note: Originally published in *Blue Clouds*.

Declaration

Sean Ramsperger

I hold these truths to be self-evident:
That no matter how many times he puts me down
I will get up each time.
No matter what he thinks of me,
We are both men created equal.
Although he underestimates me,
I know I can live up to anything.
And no matter how ridiculous his demands,
I will discount his bravado.
And let him do his own thing
So I can have life,
liberty and the pursuit of happiness.

Walls in Midair
Kai Coggin

In midair
the world changes
the borders close doors
the ports of entry bolt shut
for bodies
of specific brown
of particular religion
those who pray to Allah
those who pray to flee bombs
blowing up their children
those whose babies wash up
face down on distant shores
after flee by sea
becomes watery grave
home
is a word
that has lost all meaning
and
America (first) is
no longer
land of the free
home of the brave
a tyrant
sits on his dark throne
his maniacal pen-strokes
rob dignity
pillage dreams
rape progress
lady liberty cries patina tears
a river rolls down her thin copper dress
pools over the words

"Give me your tired, your poor,
your huddled masses yearning to breathe free"
while
in
midair
a wall is built
that will never keep us safe.

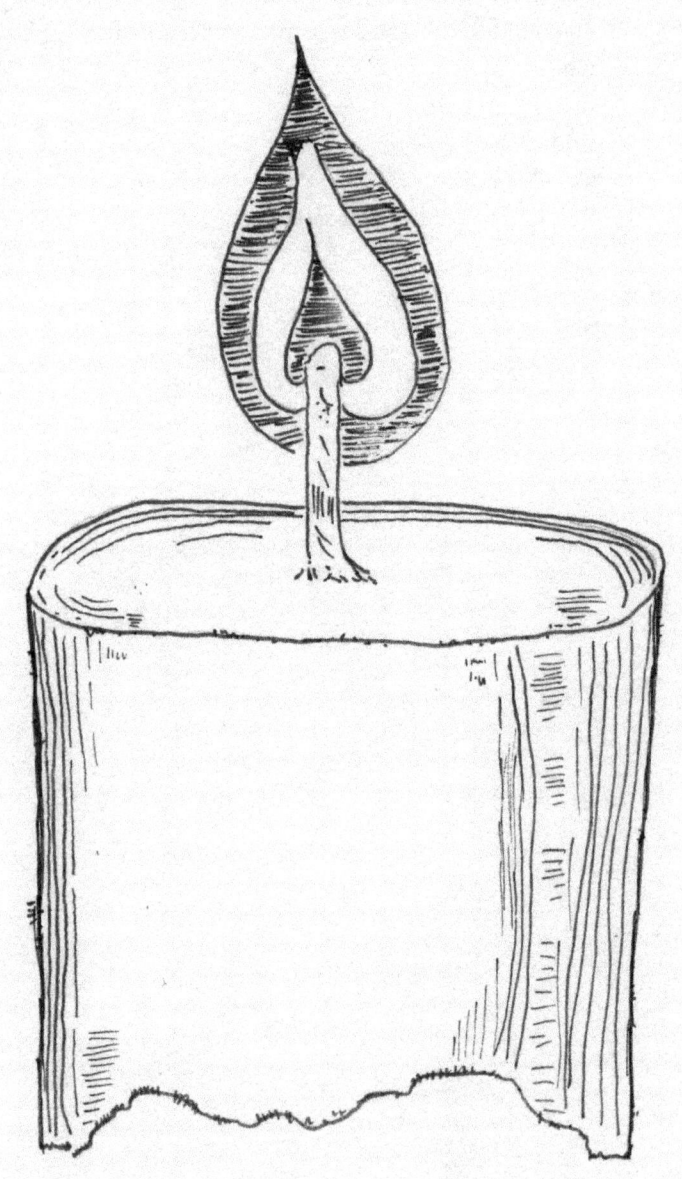

We are the light we've been searching for. ♥

CHAPTER 10

WE ARE THE CHANGE

"If one good thing has happened in America this year, it's that artists and the public have warmed up to art as a mode of resisting immoral authority."

—Barbara Kingsolver

I Will No Longer be Kept Silent
Carolyn Riker

We, the people,
on blood soaked land
crawl the borders
befallen into evil hands.

Let us be free of,
Internal bleeding,
barbed wire scars,
witnessed by elitism
unheard in
our screams from afar.

Let us be seen,
Nightfall perceives
the cries and the terrors
spirits rise,
walking the lands
gathering the courage
to speak.

Let us be known,
We, the people, died in
unlawful hands
isolated,
abolished,
penalized,
Discriminated
upon race, sex,
and religion,
marginalized,
a blood bath
lynched and beaten.

Let us rise,
A death walk of empty shoes
and bare feet
still march the earth
day and night.
Paint my skin
black, brown,
red and white
reveal the bruises of
internalized black and blue
and pain emblazed true.

There's little
liberty and justice
it has been bleached,
manipulated, raped
blinded by our
ruler's conscious
collective minds.

Let us speak,
'We, the people,'
need to be heard.
I am one more voice
and I will be speak.

Editor's note: Originally published on *The Tattooed Buddha*.

Truth and Reconciliation for Two Wings

Margo Stebbing

Dear ancestors: forgive me.
I threw you over for my white ancestors, for
you see, I was trying to survive, to feel safe,
to fit in, to walk that eternal quest of belonging
in which I have yet to reach the mountaintop,
the swale of safety and comfort,
the sense of my shoulders sinking down between the wings
of my heart,
my belly untying its knots upon knots of
anxiety because my DNA is *othered*,
my beautiful helix of amber, rice, and seashells
that I could not proudly wear until now.

My tribe of brown skin, brown eyed people, you
of kind, kind hearts, please stand at my back if
you have not walked away from your descendants
who do not even know your names,
even while I inflicted white privilege on my own
blood and being,
stepping out exactly at the crack
between the two worlds
I was forged from.

Take this roiling black sea in the pit of my stomach
and pour on it your blue sapphire seas,
the comfortable patois of your
language that I refused to learn,
the comfort of your shoulders that are not much
higher than mine, for we are a small people,

and your smiles that somehow
allow this world to make sense in all its burning.

If you are still listening,
and I know your ear is turned toward me,
I reach for you and I reach for you
as I fade into an old woman, yes, how did
it comes to this, my old years now, a life lived
without the aegis of my people, a sense of
where I fit in, the trauma I carry instead of
my belonging,
the spear that pierces a
thousand points, the trail of geese that I
look upward to the sky to hear;

The unraveling of earth as it receives their sound
in the great, lonely and haunting
return flight home,
ancestors riding the wing, you who tell me
that my DNA is now linked with stars
as well as in the interstitial spaces of
the oppressor and the oppressed that live within me.

The truth and reconciliation that births its bloody and
tear streaked way
through every cell of my body—
in the recognition of my own inner people
enslaved to the preferred dominant race
I was born into,
I ask all the white passing ways that I have lived
to bow and pray for forgiveness to this other half
that has hidden in the shadows for a lifetime,
does not even know how to call its own name,
does not even know the names
of half of my own family.

Forgive me, if I come late,
yet, still I come with

the paddles of rage and grief in both my hands—
my canoe is swift and hurtling through walls,
busting out from the nooses of fitting in,
resurrecting through the silent lynching
I have received through my life,
unspoken, unacknowledged trauma,
yet still I come to you, to myself and
the hard labor of reparation that hardly has
language or words to describe,
but only tears that would hold
the bird with two wings, though broken
learning to fly.

WHERE THE ANGELS FLY
Sonja Phillips

We have silenced ourselves so much
until we have become the silence.
Where the angels fly into the nothingness of everything.
Where the mind of god lives in the innocence of a child.

Far away from the darkness, rocking us to sleep.
For those hurts that impel us to turn to fantasy.
Even the sun has fled beyond the moon.

Here, where truth is untold;
we must seal the doors where evil dwells.
My restless spirit heeding the call of my soul.
No longer chasing ghosts in the blue skies.

My wings exhausted
My prayers unheard
[I sat down and wrote this poem].

For all of the innocent children.
I had to learn that I couldn't save everyone.
I had to learn to love beyond my fears.
Even the wind has eyes
Now that you have seen there is no unseeing.
The invisible becomes the visible.
It is only you longing for you.
One god with many names
The divine child awakens
Helping us to remember a world that we use to know
We cannot remain silent.
We are the light born of darkness.
What we think,
We unknowingly become.

Mercy
India Elaine Holland-Garnett

America is in need of mercy. Every day, in myriad ways we can do acts of kindnesses and Truth—beyond fear—with our sisters and brothers. We can, as a Nation, bring equity into each sphere of humanity. We can seek creative, innovative avenues to freely share the Love that enriches us all when we dare put aside divisions.

We are ONE.

We have history—hidden and revealed—reflected in our inhumanity shown on the very soil of those robbed through lies and treaties written in sand. We have the ability and imperative to name the injustices and to cry out for mercy locally, nationally. *Our history calls us to grow, to face the Truth and turn away from limiting, marginalizing, minimizing any and all parts of ourselves.*

Our history calls us into the bright light of day, even as we wrestle with our shameful fruits of what have been executed under the guise of Liberty. The Liberty of which we sing and about which we pledge allegiance is naked, without covering, and is shivering in plain sight!

All of us are bound by the history and all of us are free to dare live True Liberty, despite the illusion we have been asked to co-sign. We can be instrumental in the healing of our Nation, by merciful and courageous truth telling.

We can accept the unavoidable realities having been exposed and revealed to us over these past several months, as challenges to be the people of the song we sing, "America the Beautiful."

Do we have the will to accept this hard season as an "opportune moment," for loving and embracing? Or will we return to the land of make believe and false patriotism and nationalism?

Mercy,

—India Elaine

Choices
Cindy Burrill

The choices we make
To spread joy and love and hate
Our footprint on life

Empathy
BethAnne Kapansky Wright

Empathy
is the ability
to feel what
another feels
and see perspectives
beyond just
me.

And I can't help
but to try and see your way,
can't help but to try
to seek how you see—

*(though somewhere in the midst
of all that seeing,
I am left with the chaos
of too many voices,
have to take a deep breath
and re-clarify me.)*

So much anger
and hate
and rage against the machine
—and I get it
my heart hurts,
my soul hurts,
I disagree.
I worry and fear and deeply care
about what will be.

But if we don't try
to loosen all this rigidity,

then we will never
build a bridge,
build a hope,
build our light,
build our sight—
and find a means towards truth and unity.

*I love how I love
and I see what I see
—and what I see
is that our country
could use a whole
lot more
empathy.*

Surreal Reality
Robin Baldwin

The convergence of
Entering a new decade,
Raising teenage daughters,

Having no faith in a new president
Has stirred something inside me
That I don't quite understand.

A yearning to do something
To stop the ache inside my heart
Every time I read what
He is doing to this great country
Of ours that contradicts

What our forefathers fought so hard for,
What our sisters opened doors for,
What our people gave their lives for.

I am wallowing in the seas of depression
Over how many steps backward
This administration has taken us.
My daughters and all generations deserve the right to

Free speech,
Free will,
Choose who they love,
Make choices about their bodies,
Practice their religion without judgment.

We are living in surreal times of
Fake news,
Post truth,

Lies, nasty Tweets, insanity.
I am trying to hold onto hope
For our country, for each other
That we will persevere,
We will persist,
We will unite to stop the madness
Before it's too late to make a difference.

Tangible Hope
April M. Lee

I am an American, living away from America. I moved to Italy last fall, in the midst of a changing United States, and have been observing from afar my impressions of chaos and confusion, darkness and division. I am on the outside looking in, one step removed from my native country. As I experience for myself government lines and immigration issues, my awareness and understanding reach new levels. For I am suddenly a minority, afforded a uniquely fresh perspective.

Returning to a childlike state of wonder and innocence, I grapple at every turn; feeling misunderstood and less-than, different and foreign. I dared to leap, and found myself plunged into the unknown, into the unpredictable, yet perceiving and receiving all the while. Diversity and kindness, responsibility and compassion, complexity and richness.

And as I continue to assimilate and adapt, as I puzzle the previously missing pieces into their newly designated places, I ponder the challenge presented to us all. As global citizens, rather than aligning with sharply-drawn sides, do we have what it takes to work together? To break through the hurt and disconnection we are all experiencing, to bring about the serenity and peacefulness so desperately needed, to help spread love and human decency across the world?

I think we do. Just as I am being called upon to mold and shape my new existence in a shock-to-the-system startlingly dramatic manner, I think we do. And I think we must. It is time to shatter harmful and outdated beliefs with finality. It is time to openly embrace a better and unparalleled life-as-we-know-it.

This new consciousness is calling to us, and we must rise to its challenge. Painful and pernicious attitudes will begin fading with each inclusive word spoken, with each all-encompassing breath taken. Clarity and unity will begin peeking through, growing ever stronger. A revolutionary movement of tangible (not just conceptual) hope will prevail.

And the sun will surely shine, on us all, once again.

Artist Statement
Lucy M. Radatz

As a 63-year-old married white cisgender retired woman, I come in many respects from a place of privilege. No longer will I keep nicely politely quiet. Sometimes one must grow spine, heart, and conscience and speak with the Voice we are given. My survival tools since the beginning of the Implosition (begun 11/20/16) include creating with quilts, art, and writing and imagining sitting leaning against a primeval pine. The American melting pot is a flawed vision, how about being part of the American mosaic?

Editor's Note: The following art and poem were inspired by Lucy's quilts. Upon reading her powerful artist statement, seeing her beautiful, meaningful quilts, and reading the words she used to describe the symbolism behind the pieces, I was inspired to include her work in this anthology and have recreated two of her pieces into illustrations and arranged her words into a poem.

13 Stars//It Takes All 50

Words by Lucy M. Radatz

Arranged by BethAnne Kapansky Wright

Implosion.
Election.
Horrifying scream.

A flag on an old barn
that could no longer
continue to happen
in its sweet simplicity.

Broken state of
the hyper partisan
Divided States of America—
What happened to our flag
in distress and full of grief?

uneasy,
    unsafe,
        sleep…

I slowly blacked out
that painting,
the country,
our future…
then waited for what
wanted to come through.

"We" is what did.
13 stars call out
for return to wisdom
as, hopefully,
breakdown

becomes
breakthrough.

Then several months.
The Women's March.
Prayers. Bold. Be For!
Purrsist—
A pink arc moving
inexorably towards
justice.

A hopeful vision
of the United States
has ushered in for many—
It takes all 50.
It takes all 50.
It takes all 50.

Our diversity IS our unity.

INNER POET
Sonja Phillips

There is an inner poet inside of me,
She won't let me be
Now that she has awakened,
I don't think she'll ever go back to sleep.
On most lonely days I searched for her
(reaching inside of her only to find me),
Like a ghost sitting beside myself
She is always there
(that part of me no one else can see).

My unspoken prayers,
My beginnings and my ends,
An angel soothing my demons
Soaring on heavenly wings and words—
To places within.

Lurking in the mystical winds,
Both of us swept away
By lavender scented dreams…
Where the magic of poetry is born.

As my spirit awakens,
Her words bloom
Into petals, prose, and stems—
Sprouting from my lips,
Created from love's depths
So that our gifts
May someday flower humanity.

Windows
Kai Coggin

Recently
I heard
of a woman
who turned a graffitied swastika
into a window,
who connected the lines
of the hate symbol
and formed an escape route,
another thought,
a creative solution in paint.

a small hope.
a gesture against.

If only we could really open the window,
let some fresh air waft in,
see the clouds rising to remind us of our possibility,
see the flowers still in bloom though winter looms close,
yes,
but I have heard too many stories
of lines that cannot be connected,
of symbols that run deeper than blood,
of hope broken
and yellow stars reminding people
of the bleakness of what may come.

There must be something we can do,
but for now,
turn all the swastikas into windows,
add the sun shining through.

Some of Us Are Just Awakening
Maureen Kwiat Meshenberg

Some of us are just awakening
we feel the crack in our
hearts spreading wide
we feel the ache
in our souls deep
let not shame or blame
fall upon our awakening
we rise from the dark
with your torches guiding us
uniting with the infinite light
inside us
we come to our awakening
not mockingly, lightly but humbly
looking to
the ancient ones
the fervent ones
the fire starters of passion
we are awakened because
we hear the cry
and have become a part of
that cry universally
our howl merges with yours
some of us are just awakening
let us light our torch
with yours
let us burn with the
love that burns for us
out of us
through us
for a better world
I start with self
let self-hold the weaving strand

that connects me to you
I start with self
making strides within me
making strides within all
I start with self
self-love encompassing
the truth of love
we all matter to each other
expanding
aching
moving
reaching
becoming who I aim to be
more than just
steps
marches
chants
and songs
let mercy and compassion
always guide us
my evolving emerging
becomes us evolving
together
to the call of what will be.

Poet's note: This is a poem about how some of us are just awakening; and to be patient that we are taking steps for change—one step at a time.

Freedom Song
BethAnne Kapansky Wright

And what should
I do with my grief?

Should I bury it
in the ground,
cold and damp and dark,
and cover it in the recesses
of earth's cool mud?

No.
My grief sits warm
and soft and beating
—

It is much too tender
and alive to bury
in the ground,

And it tells me
this pain is
the cost of love;
that I must learn to
pay the price and be
the love I wish
to see.

And what should
I do with my rage?
Should I give it to
the wisest trees,
let them take it from me
and hold it in their
calm collective?

No.
My rage howls
with strings of fire
shooting from my tips;
much too hot and heavy,
to stay still in
calm of trees.

And it tells me to
refine rage in the flames,
so I can learn
to transform heat
and be the change
I wish to see.

And what about
my sad?
Should I give it
to the ocean? What's
one more drop of tear
in a pool of salty sea?

But my tears cling,
and tell me they don't
wish to see a sea
but me—

That their job
is to water my deep,
so I can know the
songs of the crying—
and be the compassion
I wish to see.

And what about
my numb?
The part so worn with feel,

she feels blind and
cannot see.

Do I offer her up to
the arms of a lavender sky,
let the dusky diamonds
sparkling in the night
pour light into
my darkest deep?

But no.
The stars tell me,
I must learn to open my eyes;
shine a path of hope
along life's keep.

And learn to be the light
I keep hoping that we'll be.

We Can Change Anything {{If We Choose to}}
Tracie Nichols

I wish these days
were only remarkable
for being the
first days of cicada song
this summer.

But no.

Today, yesterday,
and too many other days
mark the first morning
someone wakes up
without someone they love
in the world.

Someone whose scarlet
liquid life streamed
onto streets after bullet invaders
breached the softness of
their skin.

Their brown skin.
Their white skin.
Their ruby blood.
Our aching loss.
Our aching loss.

How can we
keep doing this?
There are voices
raised and hearts
engaged, but we
stand, ragged
and stubborn
in the chaos of our
culture's collapse
fiddling while freedom

burns and brown and
white brethren
are murdered and still
too many of us
look away as if
not seeing can
somehow stop
the madness but it
just gets bigger and
madder and bloodier.

*How can we
keep doing this?
How can we choose
inequity and hatred,
blood and death?*

We have the capacity
to change, to choose
from our still beating
hearts to step back,
to extend a hand, to
listen deeply, to
see clearly, to
love unconditionally.

We can change anything,
if we have the courage
to look ourselves in the eyes
and see the wounds
contributing to our blindness,
the hatreds planted deep
in folds of memory
by intolerances heard and
witnessed, the fears,
irrational and rational,
keeping us from embracing.

We can change anything,
if we choose to.

I choose.
Do you?

Acknowledgments

Deep gratitude to all the voices in this book.
May our truths ripple out and encourage you
to share your truths too

About the Authors

Anita Acuna is a mother, grandmother, and all the other titles befitting a woman joyfully entering the crone years. Her spirituality is ever evolving as she seeks to become more attuned to Source. She is a practicing witch, healer, and in some respects, a life coach. She has a deep affinity for nature and is blessed to be living in the Pacific Northwest.

India R. Adams is a storyteller and songwriter who has written the series *Forever, A Stranger in the Woods, Haunted Roads and Tainted Water*, and the lyrics for Forever's books. Her music and stories are about serious subjects such as domestic violence, sexual abuse, and Human Trafficking, but her characters have magnificent senses of humor. Perfectly balanced between laughter and tears, her readers see how they can empower their own perfect imperfections.

Vrinda Aguilera lives in rural, north-central Florida with her husband and three children. She works as a Montessori primary school teacher and is a poet, intuitive energy healer, and lifelong practitioner of bhakti-yoga. She is passionate about supporting others on their personal spiritual journeys and can be contacted at vrinda.aguilera@gmail.com.

Lisa Antley is from Detroit, Michigan. She currently resides in Smyrna, TN with her two daughters. Lisa is an educator dedicated to bringing the best out of her students. She enjoys family gatherings, listening to an eclectic selection of music, watching a variety of movies, taking snapshots with her camera, and being outside in the warmth of nature. Lisa's ultimate goal is to touch the lives of many through her written and spoken word.

Robin Baldwin was born and raised in Southern California, where she still lives. She writes about what's going on in her life through the views of the various roles she assumes in any given moment: mom of twins, wife, daughter, friend, manager, woman, spiritual seeker. She tries to have a positive outlook on life whenever possible, treat others like she wants to be treated, and she always wants the underdogs to win. Feel free to contact Robin through her blog *Words for Life*, www.robinbaldwin0204wordpress.com

T. J. Banks is the author of *Sketch People: Stories Along the Way, A Time for Shadows, Catsong, Derv & Co.: A Life Among Felines, Souleiado, and Houdini*, which the late writer and activist Cleveland Amory enthusiastically branded "a winner." *Catsong*, a collection of her best cat stories, was the winner of the 2007 Merial Human-Animal Bond Award. She has received writing awards from the Cat Writers' Association (CWA), ByLine, and The Writing Self.

Cindy Burrill is a mother, grandmother, self-proclaimed worrier, and admitted java junkie who has learned that there are few problems in life that can't be solved by sipping a hot latte and binging on Netflix. By day, Cindy is an Executive Assistant to the CEO of the Anchorage Museum, and by night, she whispers sweet nothings to her laptop while working towards her MFA in Creative Writing. During her free time (that she dreams of but lacks), Cindy imagines herself sitting on mountaintops and counting stars. Cindy can be reached through her well-loved, but often neglected blog www.dreamsinalaska.wordpress.com or at cindy.burrill@gmail.com.

Carmel Breathnach is a former elementary school teacher turned writer/blogger. Most of what she writes is about early mother loss and its lasting effects. In her writing she hopes to offer readers a relatable human perspective and a clear emotional thread that obliterates our differences. Born and raised in Ireland she moved to Portland, Oregon eleven years ago. She has been published in Huffington Post, Upworthy, and Scary Mommy among other publications. You can visit her blog: www.alovelywoman.wordpress.com.

Jhilmil Breckenridge is a poet, writer and activist who has spent many years being a management consultant, chef and nappy changer. She is Fiction Editor for Open Road Review, Editor for The Woman Inc., and Founder and Managing Trustee of Bhor Foundation. When not writing, she is chasing clouds and unicorns. Jhilmil is currently living in New Delhi and is embarking on a Ph.D. in the UK. Her newest project is translating and performing the work of Punjabi poet Bulleh Shah into English.

Kai Coggin is a former Teacher of the Year turned poet and author of *PERISCOPE HEART* and *WINGSPAN*. She holds a BA in Poetry & Creative Writing from Texas A & M University, and writes about love, spiritual striving, body image, injustice, metaphysics, and beauty. She just released her spoken word album debut, *SILHOUETTE*. Her poetry has been nominated twice for The Pushcart Prize, as well as Bettering American Poetry 2015, and Best of the Net 2016. She teaches an adult creative writing class and is affiliated with the Arkansas Arts Council and Arkansas Learning Through the Arts. Her website is: www.kaicoggin.com

Beverly Collier is a retired public school teacher and administrator. She's currently a Community and Social Media Anti-Racism/Social Justice Activist. Founder and Former Administrator of "Let's Talk about Racism in America". Actively campaigns for candidates that support racial and other social justice issues. Served as the facilitator for "Walk The Walk: On Being An Authentic White Ally" as part of Race, Poverty, and Social Justice Conference in Lynchburg, Virginia sponsored by the group "Many Voices—One Community."

Shannon Crossman learned the hard way that untapped creative energy casts a helluva shadow, so she crafts her sanity with her hands daily. She is a writer, speaker, gluten-free baker, and COO with a degree in Transpersonal Psychology. She is also a regular contributor at The Urban Howl. Despite her struggles with depression and anxiety, Shannon still believes in magic, craves the ocean like a land-locked mermaid, and dreams of a life without shoes.

Ilda Dashi is a former journalist/reporter, freelance writer, poet, free-thinker and freedom lover. Having graduated in journalism with a master's degree, and holding a bachelor degree in psychology, she has a rich experience of 10 years in the field of broadcasting media covering mostly the economic, political and social issues in her country of Albania. After much reflection, Ilda left these two careers to dedicate her time and energy to exploring the science of the soul, inner growth, meditation and healing. She is the author of many published poems, articles, reflections and prose in American's social media: elephant journal, The Tattooed Buddha, and GeMMagazine.

Annie Dear is my writing name and I am a wordsmith. I'm also a healing-work in process; driven to express myself in image and word. I love to share my work on my Facebook page called: Annie Dear; it's a space for joy and sorrow, pain and loss, life and growth—new friends are always welcome.

Olivia Delgado is the author of poetry and prose that she often shares on social media. Her work has been published in the *Texas Anthology: A Celebration of Young Poets*. She is currently pursuing a BA in Creative Writing with a minor in English at Southern New Hampshire University Online. Her writing often honors nature, nostalgia, family and the challenges of depression. She finds inspiration in playing tribute to the varying stories and diversity of others. She currently resides in her hometown of McAllen, TX.

Ryan Dumas is a 20-year-old disabled autistic asexual desinoromantic (only feels crushes, nothing develops beyond that) demiboy (part-boy) who enjoys reading and writing in his free time, and advocates for everyone he can. His special interest is Harry Potter and if you ask him about it, he will flap his hands and tell you all about it. He lives in Tucson and enjoys the sun though loathes the heat.

Alice Maldonado Gallardo is a Latina passionate with the power of words. Even at a young age, Alice loved words. As a preschooler, she carried a huge dictionary tome under her arms because her plan for world domination required learning a page per day. Intense curiosity and constant existential dilemmas guide her. In 2010, Alice was diagnosed with a rare autoimmune disease: Systemic Scleroderma. She was sent home to wait for Hospice bedridden and connected to a feeding tube and oxygen tanks. However, she healed and learned to walk again. She received a kidney transplant after 5 years of dialysis. You can find her driving her tiny smart car around Amherst, Massachusetts, accompanied by her elderly dog Charlie. Contact her via Facebook.

Angel Garmon is an Army Veteran and currently working in the field of Social Work. She has faced many struggles throughout her life including physical/mental abuse and the loss of many close to her, including the death of her daughter. She always used poetry as an outlet for her own process, but it wasn't until she shared one of her poems with women at a domestic violence shelter and witnessed its impact that she decided to share her gift. Since then, she writes personal poems for others, continues to write for herself, and has become a huge advocate for empowering women and plans to continue to uplift, inspire and empower through her gift of poetry.

India Elaine Holland-Garnett. Before I was born, I agreed to love; I knew then the cost would be great. I am a child of the moment; perpetually determined to embrace Justice, Mercy, Truth and Hope with every breath. I am living my dream. I am a mother and grandmother, sister and friend; a woman meeting each moment with passion and gratitude. I continue to learn what I am capable of accomplishing. Ordination by the United Church of Christ (UCC) supplied the credentials to access the dark places where broken people reside: prisons, hospitals, etc. I've attended a segregated elementary school, worked in the corporate world and learned I am no better or worse than anyone else.

Jaymz Hawkes is in his early 40s, living in Melbourne Australia. Jaymz is a man who is not afraid to shine and speak out of turn and use his voice to make a change and turn the page. To invest in an ideal and run with both feet, on the ground. He works in community health, has a loving young family (with his first child on the way). As an artist, a dreamer, a poet and a father to be, he is finding his peace by being right here and alert when needed. The rest of the time, Jaymz just wants to play as an innocence is being born, not just in the womb of his love, but here in the world, where he is no longer running away.

Nadia Iqbal is a scientist and a writer. Sometimes, she writes funny stuff. Sometimes, she writes serious stuff. She probably has too many cats though she could always use a few more.

Jennifer Jepson is married to her best friend and together they have raised two strong independent young women! She is a counseling psychologist who loves her family, running, the outdoors and a glass of wine with a good movie.

Don R. Johnson grew up in a non-believing, blue-collar Democratic Socialist family in Kansas. After spending over 20 years in religious work, he moved to the Ethical Culture movement of non-theist ethical emphasis. Long active in Social Justice Issues, he also is a lover of poetry.

Jody Kristine Johnson is a social worker and the mother of four children. She has previously self-published four books of poetry on lulu.com: *Communion* (lulu.com 2008) *Anam Cara, Poetry of the Soul* (lulu.com 2009); *Touchstones*, (lulu.com 2009); and *A Place in the Sun* (lulu.com 2012).

Jean-Louis Latil was born in 1959 in the French Alps, where he lives. He is a paleontologist and a nurseryman and he has practiced photography for over 40 years as an amateur. After years of photographing desert landscapes, he is trying to achieve abstraction.

April M. Lee is a certified holistic life & wellness coach, mentoring women of all ages. She is pleased and privileged that her clients all have one common characteristic: the courage and inspiration to take bigger leaps than they'd ever thought possible. In the fall of 2016, she pushed herself out of her own comfort zone and relocated to an Italian villa in Tuscany, where she lives full-time and will soon be hosting retreats. To learn more about April and her unique coaching services, visit her global studio at www.essence7wellness.com.

Judi Lenehan lives in Seattle with her husband and three hairy stalkers (a.k.a. cats). Talking is a form of play to her, as essential as breathing. True discussions help her learn and grow. She lost her most vocal critic yet best sparring partner when her mother died in 2014. Now, while writing, she attempts to gain a deeper understanding of both herself and the world around her. Her truth is that she envies people guided by their hearts. Hearts absorb and accept mystery. Her mind, on a good day, rolls it around and dissects it.

SK Lockhart is an intuitive poet and visual artist who worked for over a decade in post war Guatemala with survivors of the genocide. She is also a trauma therapist with a small private practice in Kentucky. In 2016, she published her first collection of poetry, *Wild Beauty: Breathing Through the Storm*.

Lauren Love is a Montessori Teacher, Intuitive Channel, Writer, Hypnotherapist and Energy Healer. She is deeply passionate about Holistic Education for Little Ones, Women's Healing and Living a Life of Love, Magic & Transformation. She is a Priestess over many lifetimes and in Service to the Re-Awakening of the Divine Feminine on Earth.

Sherry L Jonckheere is a journal and poetry writer, fine art and landscape photographer, nature lover and avid hiker. These loves sparked a permanent move from her hometown in Michigan to her heart-town in Montana. Sherry has also been a business owner and business consultant. Her willingness to live authentically, continue to learn and evolve, and stay curious brings a richness, contrast and depth to her work, relationships, and creative endeavors.

Mariann Martland is a writer, a creator. She wholeheartedly believes in humanity, love, and connection, even when she's overwhelmed by life (there's usually at least one moment each day when she feels overwhelmed by life). She writes about her personal experiences of abuse and trauma, and its impacts on her life with mental health, chronic illness, grief, loss and love. More of her writing can be found at www.MariannMartland.com.

Dolly Mahtani is a Professional Dreamer. Child of the Universe. A teacher of the RajaYoga practice at Brahma Kumaris University. A writer. A blogger. A poet. An aspiring novelist and screenwriter. A lover. A giver. An optimist, a rebel, a romantic. A breaker of paradigms and stereotypes. A spiritual social worker and activist. Her purpose and passion is to elevate human consciousness. To help people remember who they really are. You can reach her on Facebook: www.facebook.com/dolsz35 and Instagram: www.instagram.com/dollymahtani/

Maureen Kwiat Meshenberg is poet guided by her soul's journey. She is an author of *Seasons of the Soul: Transitions and Shifts of Life*. She writes for Women's Spiritual Poetry and has been published in three of their anthologies. Maureen is working on her second book: *The Distant Reach* available, 2017. She hosts sacred writing circles for women using writing as a tool for inner release. You can join Maureen on Facebook at *Heart's Calling* or at *Heart's Calling Poetry Author Page*.

Tracie Nichols, M.A. is an accidental poet exploring a sensory vocabulary, using *wordscapes* to make sense of a world that often feels overwhelming. Her poems are mostly about nature—the green kind and the human kind. Tracie is also a speaker, facilitator, and coach for highly sensitive and *multipotentialed* people trying to make sense of their world. You can find her at www.tracienichols.com.

Taylar Nuevelle is a writer and advocate for justice-involved women. She is the founder of the Who Speaks for Me? Project, which seeks to create a trauma-informed justice system for women; While incarcerated at the Corrections Corporation of America (CCA/CTF) D.C. and in the Federal Bureau of Prisons from 2010 to 2015, Ms. Nuevelle volunteered by providing legal advocacy for fellow incarcerated women. Ms. Nuevelle's writings have appeared in The Washington Post, Talk Poverty, and The Nation. You can connect with her on social media at: FB/@whospeaksforme, Twitter/@whospeaks_forme and her website is www.whospeaks4me.org/

Molly Moblo Perusse is a licensed cosmetologist with an associate's degree in Interior Design and a mosaic/mixed media artist. She is the owner/operator of A Work of Art Studio & Salon in Lakeview, MI. She is a self-taught mosaic artist of 17 years, literally using a hammer and pliers to smash glass until she learned there were specific tools for the art. Even though Molly works as a hair stylist to pay the overhead, she loves to teach and host art classes at her shop, as well as work on creating commission pieces. Molly's work can be found on her website at www.aworkofartstudio.com

Sonja Phillips is a rising poetess, a free spirit, dreamer and spiritualist. She was born in Chicago and now resides in Texas with her husband and three beautiful daughters. She has an unusual style of poetry, mystical, passionate and otherworldly. Her words are divinely inspired. She is the author of *Living Poetry: Perceptions of a Goddess* and *Erotic Papyrus: Return of the Goddess*. Sonja holds a B.A. in Spanish though her life's passion is poetry. She hopes to inspire women all around the globe to awaken to their inner goddess.

Marianne Pownall is a poet because it's the medium that gets her as close as she can imagine to the truth. Poetry cuts to the core of the human psyche, bypassing logic, and instead going straight for the jugular, heart and soul. A soulful adventurer and reckless idealist, her first love was the Holy Trinity of books, dogs and trees, and that hasn't changed. She has always been a passionate advocate of justice and equality, and a lover of all creatures, great and small. Marianne believes in fighting for the underdog and for our right to feel. You can follow her on Facebook/Blog at *Glass Slippers Hurt* and Instagram.

Julia W. Prentice is published in several anthologies: *Where Journeys Meet: The Voice of Women's Poetry* (2015), *Poetry as a Spiritual Practice: Illuminating the Awakened Woman* (2016), and *Temptation: the Seven Deadly Sins* (Lost Tower, 2016.) She holds a BA in Language and Literature, and is a Certified Peer Specialist.

Shilo Quetchenbach lives on the Northern California coast with her husband and young son, where she writes, draws, paints, and dabbles in most arts and crafts. She is passionate about exploring diversity and LGBT+ representation in fiction, in hopes that exposing young people to a wider range of ideas will help shape a more tolerant and inclusive society.

Lucy Radatz is a 63-year-old married white cisgender retired woman, who in many respects comes from a place of privilege. No longer willing to keep nice and politely quiet. She believes one must grow spine, heart, and conscience and speak with the Voice we are given. Her survival tools, since the beginning of the USA, Election or "Implosion" began on November 20, 2016 and include: creating with quilts, art, and writing and imagining while sitting leaning against a primeval pine. Her motto is *"The American melting pot is a flawed vision. How about being part of the American mosaic?"*

Kathryn Brown Ramsperger, an award-winning author, editor, and creativity coach, began her career with National Geographic and Kiplinger. She also worked for the International Red Cross and Red Crescent. Her debut novel *The Shores of Our Souls* was a semifinalist in the 2017 Faulkner-Wisdom Literary Competition and will be available summer 2017. Married and the parent of two, she's worked in Europe, Africa, and the Middle East and currently lives in Maryland.

Sean Ramsperger is a junior majoring in Economics and minoring in Asian Studies at Xavier University in Cincinnati, OH. He wrote these poems while in high school.

Cari Greywolf Rowan carries a rich, diversified history: teacher, counselor, craniosacral therapist, factory worker, journalist, bartender, and traveler. Her B.A. in American Studies and World Literature, M.A. in counseling, decades of spiritual practices and inner explorations, her daily excursions into nature gift her with fertile soil for her writing and activism.

Catherine L. Schweig is founder and director of the *Journey of the Heart Women's Spiritual Poetry Project*. She has published several anthologies by women from around the world. Her projects have grown into a vibrant online sisterhood through which women empower one another. Catherine is also an artist, lover of nature and mother who lives in Virginia with her life partner.

Nancy Shiner is a new author who has begun the journey of finding her voice. Through writing's artistic endeavors, the emotional release of boxing and the witnessing of her authentic self, she hopes to heal both adult and child whose painful past has led her here. In doing so, it would be her greatest honour if she could echo in some small part a voice for those who still battle to find the light amidst their own dark places. To witness and be witnessed, is an incredible privilege.

Margo Stebbing was born a bi-racial child in the 1950's, a social context like tectonic plates with fault lines that gave rise to a lifelong writing of poetry, engaged in social justice activism and owner of a prayer flag business in the foothills of California.

Tammy T. Stone is a Canadian writer, photographer and chronicler of life as it passes through us. A wanderer at heart, she's mesmerized by people, places and all of our wildest dreams; the world is somehow so vast and so small. She feels incredibly lucky to have been able to work, learn and live abroad, writing, photographing and wellness-practicing along the way. She invites you to see her photography and to connect with her on her writer's page on Facebook, Twitter, and her blog, "There's No War in World." Her first book, *Formation: Along the Ganges and Back Again*, published by Prolific Press, is available on Amazon.

Hillary Walker works as a psychotherapist in Alaska and loves backcountry skiing. Her work has appeared in PANK, Cirque, trans lit mag, and more.

Linda Webber is a Licensed Clinical Psychologist in Private Practice in Chicago, Los Angeles, and Anchorage for 46 years. She is a former faculty member of University of Alaska Anchorage, California School of Professional Psychology, and University of California at Los Angeles. She is an EMDR Approved Consultant, Facilitator, and Regional Coordinator, and is the co-founder of the International Institute for the Communication Arts and co-creator of the I Tunes Speakeasy Game® App "The Gift of Communication."

Jessica Wicks is a retired Public Welfare employee. She has published freelance articles for both LGBT and traditional press outlets. She currently is an avid genealogy researcher and enjoys photography. She and her wife Robin presently live in Minneapolis where they moved upon Jessica's retirement in 2000. She's active in LGBT rights, racial justice work and immigrant rights. She's currently editing a novel based loosely on her experiences living in her former gayborhood in Houston. Her go to phrases are: 'Love is love. Love is all there really is.'

Jennifer C. Zechlin is a poet, artist, and general lover of life. I am 50 years old, part of the LGBT community, and have two adult daughters. I currently reside in the Southwest US but am working toward a permanent move to the UK. Life has not always been easy, but it has offered all that is needed for me to be me and because of that, I regret nothing.

About the Editors

Carolyn (Riker) Avalani, M.A., LMHC is originally from the East Coast and transplanted to the Pacific Northwest in 1996. Carolyn has a private counseling practice and is also an educator and writing coach. She's an advocate for justice and spokesperson against racism and sexism. She's written for numerous journals and anthologies. Carolyn is a poet, a lover of music, nature and the author of *Blue Clouds: A Collection of Soul's Creative Intelligence*. Her second book of poems, quotes, prose and tidbits of wisdom is evolving under the supervision of her house lion, Copper. It is a pleasure and honor to collaborate with BethAnne, as co-editor and contributor of *Hidden Lights*, where voices and stories need to be shared and heard.

BethAnne Kapansky Wright, Psy.D., LP is a Clinical Psychologist who recently closed her private practice in Anchorage, Alaska to move to the island of Kauai, where she is planning on continuing to run a small practice and expand into new creative and spiritual opportunities. She specializes in life transitions, trauma, grief work, spirituality, and finding healing in our relationships, especially our relationship with our self. BethAnne is an artist and illustrator and the author of several books including *Lamentations of the Sea: 111 Passages on Love, Loss and Letting Go* and *Heliotrope Nights: Starlight for the Mind and Soul*. She is exceedingly grateful and happy to have combined forces with Carolyn and to have had the opportunity to be a co-editor of the *Hidden Lights* anthology project.